THE TRAVELER

THE TRAVELER

An American Odyssey in the Himalayas

Text by ERIC HANSEN   *Photographs by* HUGH SWIFT

SIERRA CLUB BOOKS   SAN FRANCISCO

LIBRARY OF CONGRESS CATALOGING-IN-PUBLICATION DATA

Hansen, Eric—
    The traveler : an American odyssey in the Himalaya / by Eric Hansen.
        p. cm.
    ISBN 0-87156-521-8: $25.00
    1. Swift, Hugh.   2. Himalaya Mountains Region—Description and travel.   3. Tourist trade—Himalaya Mountains Region.
    4. Travelers—United States—Biography.
    I. Title.
    DS485.H6H28   1993
    954.96—dc20   93-18400
                                                        CIP

Production by Susan Ristow
Jacket design by Christine Taylor
Book design by Christine Taylor
Photographs by Hugh Swift
Composition by Wilsted & Taylor
Printed and bound in China
Produced by Mandarin Offset

10 9 8 7 6 5 4 3 2 1

To D.R. with love and affection

ACKNOWLEDGMENTS

This book was realized largely as a result of the patience, generosity, and artful persistence of the Swift family. They provided the photographs and turned over twenty-five years' worth of Hugh Swift's journals without any preconditions or demands.

I would also like to thank Hugh's friends and family members who provided material and sat through interviews and dredged up memories. This diverse group consists of Pat Swift and Richard Cleverly, Charlie and M'Lou Swift, Don Cohon, Marilyn Young, Ben Ailes, Pam Shandrick, Ted and Cathy Worcester, Charles Gay and Pam Ross, Kevin Bubriski, John Mock and Kim O'Neil, Hugh Downs, Tom Dolan, Ken Scott, Ray Rodney, Robert Holmes, and Stan Armington. I would also like to thank my wife, DelRae, and friends Alice Erb, Robyn Davidson, Ted Simon, David Weir, and my editor Jim Cohee, all of whom either inspired sections of the text or read the manuscript in progress.

Fifty percent of the royalties from *The Traveler* will be donated to Seva—the foundation that is dedicated to the prevention and cure of blindness in Nepal.

OPPOSITE Monks carrying timber, Bhutan.
OVERLEAF Zanskar, Ladakh.

CONTENTS

1

WINDOWS ON THE WORLD *1*

2

A LEAF ON THE RIVER OF LIFE *13*

3

TASHI GONGMA *33*

MOUNTAIN GUIDE

4

BIG MOUNTAINS, HAPPY PEOPLE *59*

THE CHANGING FACE OF SHANGRI-LA

5

BESIDE THE PERFUMED RIVER *89*

A NOTE ABOUT THE PHOTOGRAPHS *100*

BY KEVIN BUBRISKI

1

WINDOWS ON THE WORLD

Peculiar travel suggestions
are dancing lessons from God.

KURT VONNEGUT

IN THE SPRING of 1983, I sailed from San Francisco to Sydney, Australia, aboard the P&O liner *Sea Princess*. Friends were invited to come celebrate the departure at a bon voyage party, and the invitation suggested that everyone wear cruise apparel. On the day of the event, Goodwill and Salvation Army thrift store merchandise was well represented by recent purchases of sun hats, black-framed eyeglasses studded with rhinestones, and hair nets from the 1950s. Several of the ladies wore gloves; while the men paid tribute to other timeless classics such as madras print shorts, white knee socks, and aloha shirts. Ben Ailes, the photographer, showed up in a white linen suit and a panama hat.

Hugh Swift, whom I had only met once before, arrived on the gangway dressed in the garb of a Pakistani hill tribesman: a Chitrali wool cap on his head, a long-sleeved, knee-length shirt known as *kameez,* and a pair of *shalwar*—the low-crotch, baggy pyjama pants of Asia. By coincidence, most of the deckhands on the ship were from northern Pakistan and they could hardly contain their excitement when Hugh came aboard in their traditional dress. They gathered around him as crisply uniformed British officers with ruddy cheeks looked on from the bridge. The Pakistanis were delighted to learn that the strange white man could speak their language, and I later discovered that Hugh had visited their villages and knew several of their relatives. Later on, the crush of bodies in the cabin prevented much mingling and before I had an opportunity to talk with Hugh the loudspeakers in the companionway announced that it was time for all guests to go ashore. I handed out bottle rockets and matches as the crowd funneled down the gangway.

The lines were cast off, the crowd waved, and champagne corks and exploding bottle rockets flew through the maze of multicolored streamers and fluttering confetti that filled the widening gap between the ship's hull and the wharf. The ship sounded its horn and pulled further away

be transformed by the experience. Now it is far more likely that the fragile destinations will be trampled by the crush of visitors.

Hugh continued to make his solo treks in the Himalayas and became a well-respected mountain guide. I had long since turned my interest to Southeast Asia and the Middle East, but we remained united by our earlier travels in the Himalayas. One evening Hugh recounted the time he fell into a crevasse on the Kondus Glacier in Pakistan and saved himself with an umbrella. Later, I described what happened the night a 65-year-old grandmother from New York City rescued me from a drunken Sherpa wielding an ice axe near the holy lakes of Gosainkund, Nepal. At our last dinner, Hugh told the story of how he had once stood up and sung "Why Do Fools Fall in Love" (Frankie Lyman and the Teenagers) at a traditional Tibetan wedding. At the end of that meal Hugh, who never owned a car, climbed onto his bicycle, and disappeared into the night. A year

Boudhananth Stupa, Kathmandu.

from the dock as the rocket barrage intensified. For a moment I could see Hugh, reeling from the champagne and covered in paper streamers, as he attempted to light a rocket fuse in the blustery wind. It exploded in his hand and I could see him laughing crazily as he disappeared in the crowd. The big ship rumbled past Alcatraz and slipped through the Golden Gate just at nightfall. Three years passed before I saw Hugh again.

During the weeks that it took to cross the Pacific Ocean, the deckhands would occasionally come up to me and whisper things such as "And how is our good friend Mr. Hugh?" or "We are very happy to see your friend wearing our clothes and making us think of our homes that are so far away." Although I didn't know it at the time, Hugh had spent most of his life commuting between the United States and the Himalayas. He had already walked 3,000 miles from Bhutan to Nanga Parbat in Pakistan, authored a guidebook to the Himalayan and Karakoram ranges, and

Hugh Swift with Pakistani deck hand, 1983.
Photo by Ben Ailes.

ABOVE **The way to Humla.**
OPPOSITE **Terraced fields, Bhutan.**

filled dozens of notebooks with thoughts and impressions gleaned from twenty-five years of travel. Like many others who had launched themselves into Asia in the mid-1960s, Hugh had succeeded in connecting with another culture.

Hugh and I corresponded over the years, and when we were both in Berkeley we would meet for dinner at Pasand, the Indian restaurant on Shattuck Avenue where, over *masala dosa* or Thali dinners, we sipped Taj Mahal beer and thumbed through our notebooks, exchanging the type of travel information that is seldom found in guidebooks. Tips on where to obtain an Iranian visa in Tel Aviv, the address of a money changer dealing in U.S. dollars in Rangoon, how to enter Tibet from India without the customary border formalities, as well as the address of a rubber stamp company in San Francisco that for a modest fee would duplicate the Chinese Army road permit that in the mid-1980s made possible a solo journey to Mt. Kailas, the sacred mountain in Tibet.

Woman of Laya, Bhutan.

Penciled notes crossed the tabletop describing the precise location of seventeenth-century Buddhist monasteries and tiny Tibetan communities that don't exist on any map. These hidden valleys are culturally similar to the regions of Dolpo and Mustang, but they remain "undiscovered" because the few intrepid travelers who have been there have also had the decency not to betray their location.

At these meals we also talked about the commercialization of travel and how slick marketing methods had fed a plague of adventure travelers in search of their next merit badge. The net result was big profits at home and accelerated social and economic change in places that had no means of defense or way of assimilating what was being thrown at them. The opening up of remote areas in the Himalayas to commercial tourism was irritating to Hugh, who had spent years tracking down the few remaining pristine places for the simple pleasure of being there. I can remember when the primary purpose of travel was to went by—a few postcards arrived from distant places, but I never saw or heard from him again.

On February 15, 1991, while standing on a sidewalk in Hayward, California, Hugh fainted. He hit his head on the concrete and died the following morning without regaining consciousness. Considering that Hugh had circumambulated Annapurna fourteen times, Mt. Kailas three times, and walked nearly 15,000 miles through the Himalayas without serious injury, it seemed an odd way for his life to end.

Both Hugh and I had spent most of the previous twenty years traveling back and forth across Asia. After recently looking through a box full of his diaries, I am amazed at the number of times we were in the same place within a week or so of each other: the covered bazaar at Tashkurgan, Afghanistan, in 1971; Langtang Valley, Nepal, the winter of 1973; the Street of

the Storytellers, Peshawar, Pakistan; Bugis Street, Singapore; and the village of Nyak on the upper reaches of the Buri Gandaki Valley, Nepal, in October 1974. Although I remember these places clearly, many familiar landmarks from those days are already gone. From an article in the *New York Times,* I learned that the bazaar at Tashkurgan was bombed to rubble by the Russians, and on a recent visit to Singapore I discovered that the old Bugis Street night market, with its open-air food stalls catering to an evening clientele of local residents, drunken sailors, package tour groups, and a parade of fabulously attired transvestites who rolled in around 1 A.M., had been converted into a shopping mall and fast-food version of the original scene.

Hugh and I never traveled together, but we often talked about collaborating on a book about the old overland trail from Europe and Istanbul to Kathmandu, then on to Australia by way of Southeast Asia. The huge migration of Westerners that

OPPOSITE **Tikse monastery, Ladakh.**

ABOVE **Woman with her pet pig at Gasa Dzong.**
OPPOSITE **A shrine in Kathmandu, Nepal.**

swept across this area from 1965 to 1975 was a multifaceted, nonstop road show that drew in such people as Bruce Chatwin (following in the footsteps of his hero Robert Byron), Martha Gellhorn, Baba Ram Dass (Richard Alpert), as well as renegade Guggenheim fellows, draft resisters, Tibetan scholars, junkies, mountain climbers, distinguished chamber musicians, Peace Corps workers, university professors and hookers on sabbatical, aspiring *sadhus,* trust fund gypsies, and anyone else who had the courage or inclination to throw themselves at the weirdness of the world.

For a significant number of these travelers, the trips were calculated not in terms of weeks, but in months or years. A journey of less than a year was to be avoided if at all possible, and the ease of friendships and the international flavor of the road made it effortless to keep the momentum going. A general lack of money helped produce a generation of sympathetic and resourceful travelers who seldom had

guidebooks or maps, but who kept copious notes, traded information freely, and had the presence of mind and confidence to change their plans en route. *How* one traveled was more important than *where* one traveled. The political chaos in Iran and the occupation of Afghanistan, combined with the ease of air travel and changing expectations of a new generation of more focused and affluent travelers, with less time or inclination to tempt fate or indulge their curiosity, finally obliterated the old overland route and the serendipitous style of travel that was a part of it.

What sent both Hugh and thousands of others out into the world was the social upheaval in the 1960s, particularly the war in Vietnam. As a conscientious objector, Hugh chose to teach English in Hue, and a couple of years later I was drafted and left the United States for seven years. Since we both had been brought up in the comforts of middle-class America, it was impossible not to be mesmerized by the richness and simplicity of daily life in Asia. Hugh developed what he called his bicontinental commute between Berkeley and Kathmandu, and after years of wandering I eventually came home to start writing about what had happened on the road.

Tom Robbins once wrote that "Outlaws are living signposts pointing to elsewhere." Looking at Hugh's life, I can see that he was one of those signposts—an inspiration for people to pursue their dreams and to learn how to cultivate their own foolishness. While the text is, in a way, a tribute to a generation of travelers, the photos are Hugh's legacy: windows onto an adopted world from which he never fully returned.

2

A LEAF ON THE
RIVER OF LIFE

In every parting there is
a latent germ of madness.

GOETHE

WELL-ADJUSTED PEOPLE leading ordered and sensible lives have been known to wake up in the morning with inexplicable cravings. They want to move to Tuscany or Provence, or journey the length of South America by public bus. Others dream of rowing across the Atlantic in an open boat, or walking a thousand miles through the Himalayas. Whether it be a desire to buy camels and retrace the steps of Wilfred Thesiger across the sand hills of the Rub al Khali desert of Saudi Arabia, or submit oneself to the mind-altering ordeal of discovering India by third-class rail—these visions usually pass and most people are fortunate to be able to roll over and go back to the safety of their dreams. But not everyone can resist the temptation to head for the horizon.

Contrary to popular opinion, travelers are not a unique breed blessed with divine guidance or superior genes. For the most part they are everyday people who have the persistence, imagination, faith, and whatever else it takes to pursue their vision.

The burly, ego-driven types rarely go the distance. If there is an element of "greatness" in the act of travel, it is the courage to step out of what is familiar and follow your feelings and indulge your curiosity. The most precious gift to bring back from a journey is the ability to see the extraordinary in the everyday and the knowledge that you can do far more than you ever thought possible. Most worthwhile journeys have humble beginnings. There are no brass bands, corporate sponsors, commemorative stamps, expedition flags, or movie offers. In most cases no one is even aware that you have left town, let alone embarked on a journey that will change you for life.

But where does a journey begin?

Ted Simon began a five-year, 70,000-mile, around-the-world motorcycle odyssey without a motorcycle or the knowledge of how to ride one. He was 45 years old when

OPPOSITE **Budhanilkantha (sleeping buddha), Kathmandu.**

14

Lama blessing pilgrim, Bhutan.

he left London one rainy night in search of the English Channel.

Twenty-seven-year-old Robyn Davidson's 1,500-mile crossing of the western deserts of Australia with four camels began with her arrival in Alice Springs at 5 A.M. with a battered suitcase, a dog, six dollars, no friends, no job, no camels, and no place to stay.

In 1973 a vacationing Frenchman bought a Balinese *jukung* (double-outrigger sailboat) for $200, filled the open hull with coconuts, packed food into lengths of giant bamboo, hired a local fisherman, and sailed 500 miles across the Timor Sea to Darwin, Australia, with a high school geography book and the stars as his only navigational aids.

I once met a middle-aged man who, having tired of his office job in Buenos Aires, bought a three-speed bicycle and pedaled 19,000 miles through South America.

I like to think that at any given moment there are thousands of similar trips in progress, and it is a pity, really, that we will probably never hear the details of what happened. Why did they leave? What gave them the courage to go? The reason we seldom come across accounts of these journeys lies in the fact that once people cut themselves free, it is a very difficult task to come back and try to sit down and write about it for strangers. For this reason, I am certain the very best stories will never be told.

But whether you choose to travel or not, the urge to get away is common to all of us. It may be the result of some latent sense of nomadism or a desire to redefine yourself. Travel magnifies and intensifies life. It allows you the opportunity to recapture a feeling of wonder, innocence, and youth; and depending on how vulnerable you are willing to become, it can also deliver a profound experience of unreality that can rattle your most basic beliefs. If nothing else, it is an excellent way of escaping self-imposed inhibitions, public scrutiny, and the mundane routines of daily life that we cunningly devise for ourselves.

After searching through Hugh's journals of twenty-five years, I'm still uncertain where his journey began. It might have started with the teachings of Gurdjieff and Fritz Perls, or in the poetry of Kenneth Patchen, an example of which was penciled into an early notebook:

Isn't all our dread a dread of being
Just here? Of being only this?
Of having no other thing to become?
Of having nowhere to go really
But where we are?

Hugh's diaries are filled with quotes from Jack Kerouac, Kurt Vonnegut, Carlos Castaneda, William Burroughs, Hermann Hesse, Ken Kesey, Tom Wolfe, E. F. Schumacher, Walt Whitman, and Hunter S. Thompson. The lyrics of Bob Dylan eased his way through late adolescence, but what launched Hugh into the adult world of politics and moral issues was the war in Southeast Asia. Like thousands of others, he was faced with the draft. Young men were tormented by the pressure of having to make the decision to submit, avoid, or resist; and regardless of what you did, there were serious consequences. Some of us enlisted, many left the country or found a way out, while others crumbled under the pressure and took their own lives. The toll on many of those who served is still painfully evident twenty-five years later. It is difficult to imagine a contemporary issue that would engage the country in the way that Vietnam affected Hugh's generation; and one of the sad things about the war is that regardless of whether one chose to shoot Vietnamese farmers or leave the United States, in protest, no one escaped the war in Southeast Asia. Looking back, it is sad to realize that an entire generation was manipulated by the mistakes and deceptions of our foreign policy makers. Henry Kissinger claimed that we were fighting for "negotiating strategies"—a vague concept for which few of us were willing to kill or die.

Hugh's response to the draft was made easier by the fact that he had been brought up in a Quaker family and his father had spent time in jail as a pacifist during World War II. In June 1965 Hugh joined International Voluntary Services (IVS) as a conscientious objector and went to Hue, South Vietnam, to teach English for two years. Hugh was immediately attracted to the rawness of life in Asia. The norms were radically different from what he was accustomed to, and for the first time he was exposed to a culture where art, work, play, and religion were totally integrated. It came as a great relief to escape the social scrutiny and routines of everyday life in America, and before long Hugh had loosened his grip on rigid Western concepts of self, time, comfort, and privacy. He taught English at Quac Hoc High School in Hue, and spent hours sitting on the banks of the Song Huong (the Perfumed River) watching the houseboats full of children. Hugh had a profound need to be an outsider, but he also had a gregarious side and during his visits to Saigon he headed for the bars of Khanh Hoi, the notorious dock area where black GIs drank 33 brand beer and listened to Aretha Franklin, Otis Redding, and Smokey Robinson and the Miracles. He immersed himself in the language and practiced his Vietnamese with the pedal cab drivers, prostitutes, pimps, and street hustlers of Saigon. Hugh once spent an afternoon on the beach at Vung Tau (Cap St. Jacques) drinking cold American beer while fifteen miles across the bay U.S. Navy jets dumped napalm on a village of "suspected" Viet Cong sympathizers. That evening Hugh was back in his newly adopted world listening to Sam and Dave while making moon cakes with the bar girls of Khanh Hoi in preparation for Tet, the lunar new year celebration.

Daily contact with his students nurtured his love for the Vietnamese. One of Hugh's students, Thuan, invited him home frequently, and the lanky American was quickly taken in as one of the family. Thuan and his family introduced Hugh to the simplicity and harmony of life in Asia. It was something he had never

Ladakhi man spinning wool.

experienced, and what had initially seemed like poverty by American standards soon revealed itself as an infinitely rich and varied life as part of a family and community. Hugh was quickly seduced by a way of living that was virtually unknown in his own country. The more time he spent with the Vietnamese, the more he grew to admire their courage and gentle dignity when confronted by the bloody charade that the United States was conducting against them. While Washington was busy peddling the fantasy of certain military victory, Hugh's observations, coupled with comments by the Vietnamese, American GIs, students, and foreign journalists convinced him we were losing badly. Hugh once traveled from Hue to Saigon by military aircraft and counted more caskets in the plane than the number of soldiers the U.S. government claimed were being killed in a week. The realization of what the U.S. government was doing in Vietnam changed Hugh for life and convinced him not to take part in mainstream American society. He had arrived in Vietnam a bright-eyed young man wanting to serve humanity. He left two years later, traveled across Asia, and returned to his own country—a virtual stranger.

While Hugh was working in Vietnam, a great migration across Asia was getting under way. The overland trip between Istanbul and Southeast Asia had become a rite of passage, an opportunity to pit yourself against the world, and after two years in Vietnam Hugh was primed for the journey. When Hugh left Saigon in mid-1967, it was like letting the genie out of the bottle. Overwhelmed by a curiosity to see more of Asia, he spent the next six months traveling overland to Istanbul, before returning to the United States. On his way through Cambodia, Hugh stayed in a Buddhist monastery in Phnom Penh, where he penciled this entry in his journal: "I am a leaf on the river of life." This sentence captured the essence of Hugh.

It was another world then. To be in your early twenties and traveling alone across

Asia on two to three dollars a day was like transporting yourself to another planet. In the 1960s and 1970s, it took so long to get anywhere by public buses and trains, and so many strange things happened along the way that by the time you arrived at your destination it was highly unlikely that you would be the same person who had left home. Most travelers couldn't afford to stay in nice hotels and distance themselves from the local people and their surroundings. Instead, they worked hard at learning about the language, food, religion, music, art, architecture, and history—because the whole point of being out there was to assimilate as much as possible. The random events of a day could change you for life if you let them, and this was the primary goal of many travelers.

During this time a colorful cast of characters was making its way across Asia. Escaping the predictable world of steady employment, parking meters, television, health insurance, income tax, credit cards, phones, *Time* magazine, and the

Hindu image, Bhaktapur, Kathmandu Valley.

daily news, they created a wave of humanity that set off to discover the nooks and crannies of the world. Who knows where all these people went or how the lessons of the road were later applied to their everyday lives once they came home? But many people never came back. They died, or lost their minds, or settled in their adopted countries. The sensation of pitting intense curiosity and naiveté against one set of bewildering circumstances after another was breathtaking, and I frequently found myself muttering, "My God, I hope someone is recording all this." It was easy to scoff at the otherworldliness of Asia until you got a dose of it. It was also a time when your imagination seemed to be the only limiting factor.

The days were full of little vignettes that became permanently lodged in one's memory. Everyone who was paying attention has a collection of these tales. Like the day in Delhi when an Anglo-Indian man

OPPOSITE **Ultar, Hunza, Pakistan.**

sidled up to an American woman standing on the sidewalk and opened the conversation with a heavily accented, "Excuse me, madam . . . but would you like some penis?" The woman, thinking he was offering peanuts, replied, "Plain or salted?" The look on that man's face is still clear in my mind after more than twenty years. Or the DC-3 flight from Ban Hoi Sai to Luang Prabang in Laos with Royal Laotian Airways—which, in 1971, was rated one of the ten worst in the world. They were down to three aircraft, and rumor had it that the planes were taken out of service only when they crashed and burned. As if to substantiate the airline's reputation for preventive maintenance, once we were airborne the flight attendant walked down the center aisle handing out armrests to passengers whose seats were missing them. Far below the tattered canvas wing flaps, the dense jungle seemed to remain motionless as we inched our way slowly toward the east. Before long, the French pilot wandered down the aisle

23

pouring wine from his own bottle and chatting with the passengers. He asked if anyone would like to try flying the plane—and a few of us did.

I once met a Japanese unicyclist who had spent six months pedaling from Istanbul to New Delhi. Aspiring bodhisattvas from Newark, New Jersey, attended thirty-day meditation courses in Bodhgaya, and blond *sadhus* from Newport Beach draped themselves in saffron robes and followed the ancient *yatra* trails (pilgrimage routes) to Hardwar and Rishikesh at the headwaters of the Ganges. Cambridge-bred ornithologists, dressed in starched field shirts and high on hashish, scanned the Himalayan skies with field glasses in hopes of adding rare trans-Asian migrants to their life lists, while USAID workers scurried around like rats, furtively looking for a piece of the development pie; and like the characters from *The Canterbury Tales*, almost everyone had strange stories to tell. Macrobiotic nutritionists from Switzerland, returning from the kingdom of

Hunza, in northern Pakistan, spoke about apricot pits being the key to unlocking the secrets of longevity, while car collectors from Los Angeles told rambling tales of scouring the service records of Rolls Royce dealerships in Bombay and Delhi in hopes of tracking down priceless, one-of-a-kind vehicles such as the armor-plated, sterling silver Rolls featuring a water-cooled machine gun that fired out the rear window. The vehicle had been built for a maharajah in the 1920s.

One never knew whether to believe such stories, but the mind-boggling cast of travelers and international desperadoes was a story in itself: Korean lepidopterists, Mormon missionaries, and madmen dressed in formal evening wear bicycled down roads that led to nowhere; and vagrants, sages, and ingenues rubbed elbows with mountain climbers and blind beggars on third-class Indian rail cars. There was a gay couple from San Francisco

OPPOSITE **The Mir's Palace, Hunza.**

24

who dressed up as geishas and traveled by rickshaw across India on the fabled Grand Trunk Road from Amritsar to Calcutta. They were shading themselves with parasols the day I met them at a roadside fruit stall near Agra in 1972. By then, their entourage consisted of a man on an elephant, a naked *sadhu* holding a conch shell and a trident, and a traveling poultry merchant whose bicycle was covered with so many live chickens that only the handlebars were visible.

On Hugh's arrival in Kathmandu in 1967, he discovered he wasn't exactly breaking new ground. Many Westerners had already settled in for the duration, as others had done in Kabul, Goa, Pondicherry, Bangkok, Vientiene, Georgetown, and Kuta Beach (Bali)—which in those days had one food stall with seating for five on a wooden bench. One brief visit to Kuta Beach, these days, gives a fair idea of what twenty years of catering to tourists can do to a sleepy little Indonesian fishing village.

In Kathmandu, Hugh encountered

people like Peanut Butter Harry, Fred the Fed, Tent Tom, Dharma Dan, Motorcycle Mark, English Andy, Big Ted, Original Keith, Captain David, Long Linda, Mary Cloud, Jungli Jaan, Richard Tenzing (who claimed to be a gun runner for the Kampas—the CIA-supported guerrillas opposing the Chinese Army in Tibet), and the poet and monologist Eight-Fingered Eddy.

Complementing this group were local Nepali characters. The one I remember best is the Global Emperor, who still rules over an imaginary realm from his headquarters at the Mahadev Temple in Kathmandu. Global, as he was known to the expatriate community of Kathmandu, has a singular story. Always dressed smartly in a military-style greatcoat, with a topi perched on his head, Global was best known for his cameo performances as Himalayan sage. Back in the late 1960s, when Hugh first met him, he was much younger and more capable of getting around and expressing himself. He was a profuse scribbler on the back of cigarette packets or any kind of discarded paper he could find, and he always carried a bag full of his "writings." Five-inch by 7-inch pictures of gods and goddesses were obliterated with his disjointed comments on the *dharma* along with instructions on how to worship the different deities of the Hindu pantheon. The notes were cryptic, and few people ever got through them with a clear sense of what the purpose of the message was. He wrote in English script but his Nepali ballpoint pen pretty well precluded a sufficient level of legibility to make sense of the writing. At the conclusion of his "reading," he would give a smart salute and a nice *Namaste* before handing over the words of wisdom. Then, in the most roundabout sort of way, he would make it known that he was not against some sort of gratuity. A 5- or 10-rupee note was the going rate.

Global is a demarcater of how things have changed in Kathmandu in the last twenty-five years. By the late 1980s Global had succumbed to the video

The Global Emperor.

telecommunication revolution. Now if you ask him to discourse on the *dharma* or one of the Hindu epics such as the *Ramayana*, he will write down the title of his video clip that covers the subject and then direct you to the local video shop where Global Emperor T-shirts are also on sale. For this service he still expects a 5- or 10-rupee note.

Hugh was drawn to these sorts of characters during this first journey across Asia, so by the time he returned to the United States in 1968, after a two-and-a-half-year absence, it wasn't easy to reintegrate with his own society or his faded memory of who he had been when he left. In fact, he didn't bother trying. Instead of settling into conventional American life he began a ten-year cycle of taking unpleasant jobs for the sole purpose of financing his many trips back to the Himalayas. On his return from this first trip across Asia, Hugh moved into an apartment on the Lower East Side of Manhattan and took a job

OPPOSITE Gyaru Village, Dhaulagiri, Nepal.

with the Department of Social Services. This arrangement allowed him a perfect opportunity to alienate himself from the mainstream and develop his sense of being a fringe dweller in his own country. After the liberating experiences of Vietnam and Asia, Hugh felt trapped in an alien culture.

By day he spent his time employed at the task of tracking down fathers who had left their wives and children to the mercy of programs such as AFDC (Aid for the Families of Dependent Children); and the accounts of his forays into the bowels of Manhattan and the South Bronx, in search of absentee fathers, are far more surreal and frightening than any journey he took in Asia. Hugh got into the habit of trekking the length of Manhattan at all hours of the day and night. He was mugged once, but the incident merely fed his growing appetite for the unknown. Long before he had ever heard of Mt. Kailas or the ice lingam in Amarnath Cave, he was already making pilgrimages in

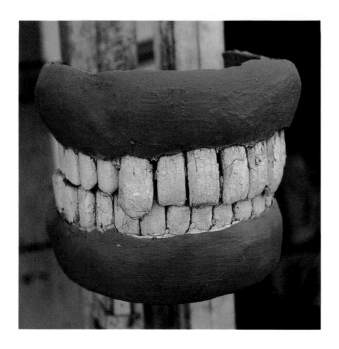

Dental shop, Peshawar, Pakistan.

Manhattan. One of his earliest ones was to the Apollo Theater in Harlem, where he took in the Saturday midnight show of James Brown.

Hugh's quest for dark corners was probably an outgrowth of his visits to such obscure places as the old Times Square Record Shop—formerly located on the subway level of 42nd Street and Times Square. Hunched over aisles of dusty bins, he spent hours flipping through used records in search of treasures such as "Stormy Weather" by the Five Sharps. His idea of a good day at the bins was the discovery of the doo-wop classic "The Paragons Meet the Jesters"—in mint condition.

Hugh's encyclopedic mind stored the names of obscure rock and roll and rhythm and blues artists and names of obscure record labels in the same way he later compiled a bewildering collection of visual and verbal clutter from his travels in Asia. In the tradition of the Global Emperor, Hugh was an archivist, a compulsive note taker, and an insatiable collector of the odd and unusual, a human trash compactor of press cuttings, overheard conversations, ticket stubs, matchbox labels, and any other scrap of information that might touch his sense of the absurd. Esoteric cross-cultural data and geographical tidbits about remote and inaccessible regions in the Himalayas were his specialty. Those early expeditions to Harlem and Times Square helped him develop his appreciation for the odd juxtaposition of images and meanings in daily life. He assembled trail information and wrote his guidebooks the way he put together his vintage record collection. That is—by bits and pieces. Like the rest of us, Hugh was a product of his own reality.

Partially fueled by a fear of being committed to any one place, Hugh worked hard at not making a settled life for himself by hopping from one culture to the other. After he moved out of Manhattan, he painted houses, worked in warehouses, and took odd jobs in Connecticut, Colorado, and California in order to buy travel

Jackal Wine, Annapurna region, Nepal.

time in Asia. In 1980, after a decade of commuting between the Himalayas and Berkeley, Hugh began working as a professional guide for adventure-travel companies in the San Francisco Bay Area. He found regular work taking small groups to the mountains of India, Pakistan, and Nepal, which he had spent the previous ten years exploring. This allowed him to integrate his life and work for the first time and to break out of a disconnected cycle of work and travel. From a distance, it seemed like a harmonious arrangement. Hugh continued his solo travels between leading trips, and during his seasonal residence in Berkeley he found time to write his guidebooks and later started work on a collection of stories about his life in Asia. Hugh had mastered the fine art of being the perpetual house guest and visitor, but those close to him could see the dilemma faced by the aging traveler who, at age 47, could no longer thumb his nose at the passing years.

It is a blessing to feel at home everywhere, but Hugh eventually came to the realization that by leading his double life he didn't feel at home anywhere. The mad serendipity of his early travels through the mountains and backroads of Asia had been pretty well reduced to mail order adventure fantasies listed in glossy brochures, and the Himalayan guides who first took Hugh into the mountains had become old men with grandchildren. After nearly twenty-five years on the road, he wanted a change. It was an easy matter for Hugh to begin a journey; the problem was in learning how to stop the process. He longed for things that many of us take for granted— the very things he had spent most of his life avoiding—intimacy and a sense of place.

3

TASHI GONGMA

MOUNTAIN GUIDE

The idea is to go totally unprepared . . .

PAUL FUSSELL

In each of our lives, certain unique
days or events shine like grand demarcations.
Birth, death, decision, love, liberation.
These experiences rise like Everest above the
meadows, meanders, and rocky hills of daily life.

HUGH SWIFT

The art of Himalayan travel—
and indeed of all adventure—is the art
of being bold enough to enjoy life now.

W. H. MURRAY

ON THE WALLS of his apartment in Berkeley, California, Hugh hung the portraits of his guides. Men such as Guda Ali, Karma Chumbey, Tensing Gyastso, Balbir from Lulang, Ghulam Nabi, and Tashi Gongma. I admired the fact that Hugh treated his guides like friends and gave them full credit for the success of his trips into the Himalayas. With the exception of Tashi Gongma, I could never recall where the other men came from or what importance they held for Hugh. But then Hugh had a wide range of friends and a huge capacity for remembering details. As a compulsive chronicler of the odd and unusual, he kept meticulous notes on pieces of folded paper that he filed in his shirt pocket. These scribblings helped him recall the details of a journey and the people he met along the way. Part seasoned traveler and part pilgrim, his pulse would quicken at the mere mention of places such as Babaghundi, Konka Wang Po, Chumarkhan Pass, Karma Ding, or Tinkar Lepu La. These places, like the names of his guides, would draw blank stares from all but the smallest handful of Himalayan travelers.

The only reason I remember Tashi Gongma is because Hugh had once spent an entire evening telling me the story of their eighteen-day trip with two pack-horses and a few burlap sacks full of supplies for the journey from Manali to Leh in northern India. The journey took place in 1989, but it was typical of dozens of other trips Hugh made from the late 1960s until his death in 1991. After more than twenty years of walking in the Himalayas, Hugh had long since refined his style of travel. By the mid-1970s most early trans-Asian travelers and intrepid trekkers had either settled in their adopted countries or gone home to digest what they had seen and done. While these people were busy applying the lessons of the road to their professions, families, and businesses, Hugh was still hopping from country to country rack-

OPPOSITE Tashi Gongma, mountain guide.

ing up the miles and going further afield. For Hugh, a voyage of discovery was not a cerebral exercise; it had to involve foot-work. This constant movement was partially an attempt to avoid entrapment in his own culture, but more significantly he felt that by returning to familiar and exotic places he might be able to recapture the sense of exhilaration and adventure from his first trips. With the passage of time, those early journeys became the most important reference points of his life.

Hugh was a meticulous planner and preferred to be as self-sufficient as possible. Common sense and years of experience had taught him that simplicity, frugality, and patience produced the most worthwhile journeys. In his effort to travel like the local people as much as possible, he would hire a guide who was familiar with the area and then disappear into remote and largely uninhabited mountain regions for weeks or months at a time. His idea of proper clothing and equipment for a month-long trek consisted of little more

than three sets of underpants and socks, a pair of *shalwar* (the baggy pyjama pants of Asia), a wool cap from Chitral, leather boots, an umbrella, and a sleeping bag. For a man who guarded his privacy at home by compartmentalizing most of his friends, these walks in the Himalayas represented a sort of liberation, because the type of contact he nurtured with his guides and strangers produced short, uncomplicated and intense friendships; the kind that Hugh had difficulty finding in his own culture. The journeys also permitted him to indulge in a unique sort of purposeful oblivion that we all dream of: a return to the self made possible by an escape from the familiar preoccupations of everyday life. He thrived on the startling beauty of the Himalayas, and one of Hugh's greatest pleasures was in not knowing for certain where he would spend the night.

Hugh was introduced to Tashi Gongma by Dhundu Ram, a horse contractor from Manali whose operations covered the western edges of the Tibetan plateau, including the regions of Lahoul, Rupshu, Zanskar, and Ladakh. Toward the end of summer in 1989, Hugh and Dhundu Ram arrived in the village of Jispa, a day's drive north of the bazaar town of Manali in the Uttar Pradesh region of India. They were having trouble finding a mountain guide with horses who was willing to take Hugh over the high passes to Hemis Gompa, a Tibetan Buddhist monastery situated on the upper Indus River basin in Ladakh. The snows could come at any time, and the men they approached were worried that if they took Hugh to Ladakh they would run the risk of being trapped there for the winter or would have to spend all their wages bringing their horses back home by truck. Just the previous year Thundup, a man from Jispa, had run into a snowstorm late in the season and was lucky to make it home in a forced march over several days.

Following a maze of irrigation ditches and stone fences, Dhundu and Hugh arrived at Tashi's home at dusk. The leaves of the cottonwood and walnut trees rustled

In the Manaslu area, Nepal.

**Bishnu and her daughter Juni,
Marpha Village, Nepal.**

in the chill air as the two men removed their shoes and climbed the wooden steps to enter a modest adobe structure surrounded by wheatfields. Once inside, the smell of sheep and goats stabled on the ground floor mingled with the acrid scent of woodsmoke, butter, and raw wool. Tashi was dressed in cream-colored homespun pants and a weathered brown jacket cut in the style of a Western sports coat. He kept a large sewing needle stuck into the lapel of his coat and wore a dark cap with white piping on the turned-up brim. Hugh was immediately attracted by the man's warm smile. Tashi, at age 58, lived with his wife, Yangzin, a teenage daughter, Tsering, and two sons, Dorje and Namgyal.

While Tashi, Dhundu, and Hugh discussed prices and the details of what supplies to bring on the three-week trip, Yangzin served tea and later a simple soup of turnips thickened with *tsampa,* roasted barley flour. Nothing was decided that night, and as the cooking fire died down the family got ready for bed. After the house had quieted down, Hugh went outside to relieve himself. A bitter wind blew down the valley, and stars sprinkled the night sky from mountaintop to mountaintop. In the morning, the two sons were laughing, and Hugh asked them what was so funny. "We are wondering," they said, "why you peed in our turnip patch last night." Hugh laughed, and then apologized for his mistake.

The negotiations lasted until midmorning, when everyone finally settled on a fee of $14 a day. Tashi would cook, guide, and provide two packhorses, Bara and Chota ("the big one" and "the little one"). The terms of the agreement stipulated that half the fee was to be paid in advance, while the second half, plus a tip, would be payable at the end of the journey. For supplies they took tsampa, wheat flour, potatoes, onions, instant soup mixes, milk powder, cashews, walnuts, dried vegetables and apricots, rice, butter, lentils, and cheese.

Dhundu Ram departed on the midday bus headed for Manali with an undisclosed share of Tashi's fee, but before the trip could get under way Hugh was asked to take pictures of the family. First they posed knee-deep in a field of flowering potato plants; then the daughter rearranged her waist-length braided hair and Hugh took a portrait of her cradling a pet pig in her arms. The younger brother Dorje, dressed in a Giants T-shirt, stood next to his mother, who was dressed in a long black robe tied at the waist with a pink sash. They were followed by older brother Namgyal, who waded into the potato field dressed in a denim jacket and a pair of pink wraparound sunglasses. He struck a haughty pose for the camera with his hair slicked back in imitation of the pictures of Hindi movie star gangsters that were pasted to the wall by his bed.

While the photo session was in progress, Tashi went off to fetch his horses. He returned some time later, leading two black geldings marked with patches of white on their backs and legs. Ola (Bara) was 12 years old and Kasseh (Chota) was 9. Dorje held each hoof in turn as Tashi replaced the old horseshoes. Tashi made a few last-minute repairs to the wooden pack frames and while he was doing so Hugh watched a 100-truck army caravan laboring up the valley. From the vantage point of Tashi's front steps, the trucks seemed to belong to a different century. They were carrying military supplies to the far north where the Indian and Pakistani armies were skirmishing over an uninhabited glacial region near their ill-defined borders with China. While the trucks lumbered up the road, Tashi and Hugh made their final preparations for their three-week journey by foot.

On the morning of their departure, Yangzin placed dabs of butter, or *tashi yarkha,* above the right ear of both Hugh and Tashi to protect them on their journey. Using the needle from his lapel Tashi stitched up their provisions in burlap sacks and then loaded them onto the horses,

which were waiting patiently. Tashi's family wished them a safe journey, then wandered off to harvest peas as the two men started up the valley past a whitewashed wall strung with multicolored prayer flags.

Glancing down the valley, Tashi pointed out a patch of rock rubble that marked the spot where his former village had been swept away by an avalanche in 1955. This was near the site where the Indian government was planning to install a 175-megawatt dam on the Bhaga River. The dam, if built, would flood Jispa and the other small farming communities further up the valley. A few miles beyond Jispa, they joined the asphalt road north, and for the next four days they spent their time dodging truck traffic and visiting with the road workers. The Sikh drivers, working their way through the gears, spewed clouds of exhaust and unburned diesel fuel over the travelers while waving to them with grease-blackened hands. A portrait of

OPPOSITE **Zanskar, Ladakh.**

the Sikh prophet Guru Gobind Singh was painted on the door of a truck that pulled over to ask Hugh where he was going and the purpose of his journey. Learning that the two men were bound for Hemis Gompa, the driver insisted that Hugh and Tashi leave the horses behind and come with them. Hugh thanked the men, but refused their offer by explaining he was *paydal yatri,* a foot pilgrim. "Pilgrim to where?" the driver asked, nodding his head from side to side. Hugh pointed to the mountains and the man laughed before driving on.

Tashi and Hugh were well matched in temperament and in their simple approach to travel. Tashi's camping gear consisted of a burlap sack that held a tarp, a kerosene stove, enamel plate, pressure cooker, wool blanket, and a round steel plate for cooking *chapattis.* While some people's idea of a wilderness experience is cheap champagne or an open window at a Howard Johnson's Motor Inn, Hugh's concept of luxury was a clean pair of socks and enough roasted barley flour and hot tea to make it over a 17,000-foot snow-covered pass to the next pristine valley or remote wasteland of unparalleled beauty.

Tashi was the sort of man who, when confronted with practical concerns such as a lack of firewood, would reassure Hugh with comments such as "Oh, don't worry. There is plenty of dry yak dung to burn along the way." On their first day out, Hugh inquired about the possibility of getting caught on one of the passes in a snowstorm. This was shrugged off with "Well, you know, last year five Bengalis froze to death up there, but if things turn nasty we can always get the Zanskari men to get us through with their yaks." Thoughts of what Tashi might consider "nasty" was enough to moisten a brave man's armpits. He was not the sort of man who was overly concerned with destinations, and for that reason alone he made an excellent traveling companion.

In Hugh's journal from the trip, I found a quote from Michael Aris, the Himalayan-

Tibetan scholar and husband of Daw Aung Saw Suu Kyi, the Burmese dissident and winner of the Nobel Peace Prize in 1991. His comment captured the central purpose of Hugh's travels:

> Sometimes, however, it seems that journeys are undertaken for their own sake, with the intention of turning anything encountered on the road into a means of spiritual profit. This is best expressed in the phrase *gang shar lam khyer*—to bring to the path (to enlightenment) whatever may happen. The journey is itself therefore regarded as being of equal importance to its goal.

Tashi's interest, on the other hand, was of a more practical sort and focused largely on the fee he would earn. But like most of Hugh's journeys, the walk allowed both men the opportunity to look into each other's changing worlds, and for a brief time become confidants and friends. During a stop to water the horses, Hugh learned that Tashi had been a farmer all his life, but for the previous eight years had taken part-time jobs leading Westerners into the mountains.

They made their first camp at 12,000 feet in a meadow well above tree line. The meadow in which they camped was known as Patseo, the Stone Bridge. Once the site of a month-long summer trade fair that flourished until the Chinese invasion of Tibet in 1951, the meadow had attracted merchants and their yak and sheep caravans from Leh and Sinkiang Province in China. Tibetan nomads, known as Drokpas, wandered in to drink *chang* and *arak*, gamble, and trade rock salt and bales of sheep wool for barley, corn, and wheat brought up from Manali on horses or mules. When Hugh and Tashi arrived at Patseo, the place was deserted apart from two immaculately outfitted geology students from the University of Lausanne. The Swiss undergraduates were gathering rock specimens and examining the terrain with the use of satellite photos. Their guide was suspicious of their work, and he later took Hugh aside to ask if

Balti men making butter at 13,000 feet.

the Swiss students were planning to sell the rocks when they got home. Hugh told the man he thought that was an unlikely possibility.

Two days up the road, Hugh and Tashi reached the Baralacha La (*La* means mountain pass). At a rock cairn bristling with fluttering prayer flags, they stopped to call out, "*So, so, so, so lha gyalo!*"—The gods have triumphed! This is the traditional phrase that travelers recite when reaching a pass in the Himalayas. It was also at the Baralacha La that Tashi threw out the 5 kilos of soggy onions that Hugh had inadvertently stored in a plastic bag. They moved on to set up camp in a windswept highland valley where Sarchu Serai, an old caravan stop, lay in ruins. Friends of Tashi were already camped there in big canvas tents that the men had set up inside the remaining stone walls of the buildings. The men warned Tashi about the weather, but he responded by shrugging his shoulders and making tea over a yak dung fire. The fire was directly upwind of where

Hugh had set up his new tent, and for the rest of the trip it held the peaty smell of burned yak dung. They hobbled the horses and camped for the night.

Shortly after sunrise on the following morning, they left the vehicle road for the last time and started up a side valley from where a milky glacial stream flowed between slopes of dark brown scree. The main trail headed north but Hugh decided to make a detour up the Tsarap Valley (the major tributary of the Zanskar River) in hopes of delivering a photograph to a man named Ngotup, whom he had met in a nearby valley years earlier. In the distance, precarious log bridges spanned narrow side valleys where streams cascaded between the sheer rock walls. After a lunch of *chapattis* and cashew nuts, they wandered along a seldom-used track high above the river where magnificent snow-covered peaks seemed to rise up in all directions as they gained altitude. At the end of the day, Hugh set up the tents as Tashi sprinkled kerosene on a pile of yak dung, applied a

match, and soon had their dinner of rice and *dal* bubbling in a pot.

The two men rarely deviated from their basic daily routine. Up at first light, Tashi would prepare chapattis and tea for breakfast each morning. Tashi boiled the tea leaves for a couple of minutes before pouring out strong steamy cupfuls of sweet milky tea. The chapattis were patted out by hand and grilled on a heavy sheet metal disk. Folded like crepes, the chapattis were filled with cheese or jam, or eaten plain. After discussing the plan for the day, Hugh wrote in his journal while Tashi prepared a treat for the horses. He called it *chak*—a stiff dough mixed with leftover tea leaves and molded into a ball. They would then break camp and load the horses, and before the sunlight had started to creep down the hillsides the little entourage would be moving along the narrow trail. Lunch was a simple affair of more tea and leftover chapattis from breakfast, with dried fruit and nuts. By late afternoon they would select a camp near water and then turn out the horses to graze while Tashi prepared dinner.

Days later, Tashi and Hugh were coaxing the horses up a narrow path along the valley walls. They could not find any water, but before long it began to rain and small rivulets provided them with something to drink. Rain clouds spread a gray light across the narrow valley far below, muting the rich yellows and greens of ripening barley fields. At the edge of the fields, Hugh could make out the cluster of low stone houses that marked the village of Satak. They arrived in a downpour, anticipating a break from the miserable walking conditions, but to their surprise no one invited the travelers in for tea or *chang* (a fermented barley beer) and Ngotup, the man they had walked for three days to see, was nowhere to be found. Tashi laughed at the unusual lack of hospitality, and they continued on. At midday they decided to set up camp at a place called Mone Leh, which consisted of a deserted stone shelter surrounded by abandoned terraces. The

track was too rough to take the horses further, but Hugh continued up the valley on foot toward a hot spring called Chutsan Naga. Two men dressed in magnificent wool robes trotted by on horseback and called out, "Come bathe your stiff, gimpy legs." Hugh waved politely, but declined their invitation. Instead, he examined the ruins of an ancient nunnery and then walked to the villages of Yurshoon and Murshoon (upper and lower Shoon). At Yurshoon he was given tea, tsampa, butter, *churupe,* and *darra* (buttermilk) by a man whose name he never learned.

In neighboring Murshoon (20 minutes further on), Hugh explained that he was in search of Ngotup from Satak—the man in his photo. He was led to an old woman who was elbow deep in a pot of red dye extracted from a mountain shrub. This was Ngotup's ancient mother. Like the other women of Ladakh and Zanskar, she was dressed in a maroon cap and an ankle-length robe known as a *cos.* She had thrown a goatskin over her shoulders, and puckered leather soles protected the bottoms and sides of felt boots that peered from beneath the hem of her robe. The woman glanced at the color photos of her son as if they were nothing out of the usual and then announced that her son was in the high pastures with his yaks. As a present, Hugh handed the woman a very large sewing needle, which produced a far greater response than the photograph. "Now *here* is a present!" she seemed to say with her eyes. In return, she gave Hugh a double handful of *churupe*—a crumbly, sun-dried cheese made from yak milk. Three nuns with shaved heads and maroon robes were present, and to these women he distributed photos of the Dalai Lama. They touched the photos to their foreheads in a gesture of respect then asked Hugh if he would like to buy some of their home-made *arak*. Arak is a notorious distilled liquor known throughout the Himalayas for its potency. At 25 rupees each, Hugh bought two bottles.

"Rather strong it was," Hugh noted in

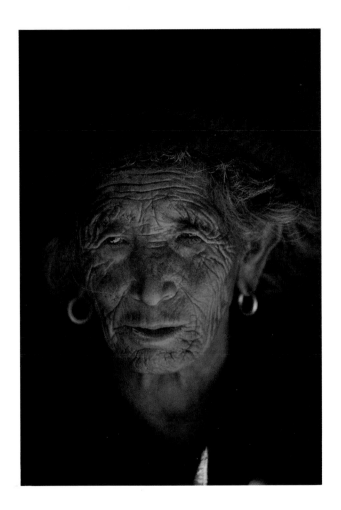

Tibetan woman, Annapurna, Nepal.

his journal. "Could have tasted better, but I managed to drink about ¾ of a bottle with the nuns before staggering out into a fresh downpour." Hugh ducked into the house next door and drank chang with another family until the rain started to let up just before sunset. Hugh took photos of the family with an empty camera, and then it was time to leave. On the way back to camp, he stumbled down the trail in an altered state that rapidly disintegrated into a drunken stupor. Before long it was dark, and Hugh was lost. He moved along the slopes without a flashlight, crossing streams and floating down the invisible trail without missing a turn or stumbling. Gripped by the arak, he could have ended his walk in tragedy, but Hugh was too preoccupied to consider the possibility of danger. Immersed in a vision of Lungta—the sacred Tibetan wind horse—he then shifted his thoughts to a story told by Lama Govinda and Alexandra David-Neel about the mythical *lung-gom-pa*—people from Tibet who could walk at superhuman speed. Hugh stopped in the darkness. "*Lung-gom-pa,*" he exclaimed, pounding his chest with his fist.

Lung-gom-pa means "spirit, or trance walker," one who, in a mystical state, can cover incredible distances. Moving down the valley and through an assortment of visions, Hugh saw the Hindu deity Shiva dancing madly across the star-filled skies with Little Richard. Then Hank Ballard appeared in maroon robes, twirling a prayer wheel and singing "There's a thrill upon the hill" (a line from the song 'Let's Go, Let's Go, Let's Go'). Hugh eventually caught sight of a distant fire. He didn't know for certain how long he had been walking or where he was, but some internal homing device or sense of survival had led him in the right direction. As he drew close to the fire, it was clear that Tashi had been worried. He asked what had happened, but when Hugh showed him the half-empty bottle of arak Tashi just laughed and muttered the word "*Gesar.*"

The Ladakhi Gesar legend to which

Tashi was referring recounts the adventures of a far-ranging mythical hero, Gesar, who with divine guidance wandered over the mountains and countryside combatting evil spirits and protecting the lives of the people he met along the way. In Hugh's brief role as Gesar, the demons he encountered were of his own making and if credit for his safe arrival could be attributed to the gods, it would be due to the god of arak.

During their stay in Mone Leh, Hugh witnessed a sight that added a sense of urgency to their journey. Overnight the Tsarap River changed color from milky gray to a light blue. The glaciers had stopped melting, and this was the first tangible evidence that the seasons were changing and the snows would soon arrive.

The next day at Satak they ate lunch in a one-room hut that was home to one-toothed Tashi Namgyal. His well-patched woolen clothes were all the same color of faded brown, and the man's hospitality was extended to the mice who scurried fearlessly about the floor picking at food scraps during the meal. Here in Satak, Hugh was forced to switch from his basic Hindi to a scattering of Ladakhi and Tibetan words because no one understood Hindi this far from the road. That afternoon they left the main river valley and entered a narrow cleft in the mountains that led to the Marang La. At 17,350 feet, the Marang La marked the boundary between the regions of Zanskar and Rupshu. It was also the highest pass on the trail to Hemis Gompa. Rupshu lies at the western edge of the Tibetan plateau. The only people who inhabit the area are the Changpas—nomadic herders—who live in canvas or yak hair tents while tending their animals during the summer months.

Hugh was still working off his arak hangover as he strode past Tashi and the staggering horses on his way to the top of the Marang La, which was covered with patches of old snow. The snowy peaks of Zanskar lay behind, while cloud shadows rippled across the barren terrain of

Rupshu that opened up before him and extended to the eastern horizon. They traveled for three or four days without seeing anyone. One camp was named Chu Mindu (no water), and another Shing Mindu (no firewood). The landscape through which they traveled was utterly desolate and mesmerizing. Dense white clouds flew across cobalt skies by day, while at night the clouds were transformed into dark shapes that drifted over a field of glittering stars.

These days of solitude were broken the afternoon they encountered a young farmer by the name of Tsewang Doriah. He was busy harvesting a measly-looking crop of barley, and apart from exchanging the briefest of greetings he paid little attention to the travelers who had appeared out of nowhere. Hours later, and several miles up the trail, where Hugh and Tashi pitched camp, they were surprised to see a man on horseback riding up the valley in the fading light. As he drew near, they noticed he was dressed in knee-high boots with a magnificent maroon robe and a fur cap. When the man reined his horse to a halt and dismounted, both Hugh and Tashi were astonished to discover that this vision of Genghis Khan was the young barley farmer they had passed earlier. He had changed into his best clothes to pay the two strangers a visit. They offered him tea, and during the conversation Hugh learned that for the last five days they had been in Karnak—the western region of Rupshu. The area was similar to the high, rolling plains that Hugh had recently traveled through north of Mt. Kailas, the sacred mountain in western Tibet.

Tashi produced a package of cream-filled cookies from his burlap sack, and Hugh brought out the second bottle of arak. Beneath the darkening sky, they huddled around a fire of yak dung, telling stories and drinking arak. Later on, the horseman reached inside his coat and pulled out a gift of leathery pieces of sun-dried meat. Hugh was so impressed by the horseman that he asked if he could take the man's picture. He did so and later, when the man got up to leave, Hugh handed him the rest of the cookies and asked for his full name and address so that he could send a copy of the photo. "Tsewang of Karnak," the man replied proudly as he climbed into the saddle. Without another word, he spurred his horse and disappeared into the night. The sounds of hooves soon faded in the distance and they never saw the man or their package of cream-filled cookies again.

Traveling through the deserted valleys of Rupshu, they encountered dramatic *mani* walls made from thousands of stones inscribed with the mantra "*Om mani padme hum.*" Clusters of whitewashed *chortens,* strung with prayer flags, were set like gigantic chess pieces between the barren hills. Across the dry river bed, a group of abandoned stone shelters blended into the contours of the hillside as ibex clattered up rocky slopes and riders on horseback rippled in the distant heat shimmer, only to vanish minutes later as clouds moved in and an eerie rain began to fall.

Resting the horses, Tajikistan.

Hugh was looking forward to arriving in Sangtha, the first village in Rupshu, but when they entered the town they discovered it was deserted apart from an old geezer and his two donkeys. Most of the villagers were either to the north in the pastures near Zara or further east tending their herds in the grasslands of the Chang Tang. The others were still in the upper pastures, near snowline, tending the yaks. Continuing on, the country opened up to reveal scattered green patches on the hills to the north. The trail contoured a set of gentle, rolling hills to the west that gave sweeping views of distant river valleys and mountains. In a sheltered valley, they came upon hundreds of sheep and goats tended by two girls, four boys, and a bronzed old woman. Two of the boys, dressed in wool robes and blue, high-topped Chinese tennis shoes without socks, performed an impromptu dance and then asked for cigarettes and pens. Hugh handed them a picture of the Dalai Lama.

Mesmerized by the succession of valleys and passes, Hugh began to lose track of the days. Atop Yar La, he remembered clouds blowing across the surrounding mountainscape dappling the endless expanse of rock with cloud shadows. The extreme contrast of light and shadow dazzled Tashi's eyes and Hugh lent him his extra pair of glacier goggles. Days later, as they stumbled on the nearly deserted village of Dett, Tashi continued up the trail to make camp while Hugh explored the village. Walking down a laneway carpeted in sheep pellets, he spotted smoke leaking from the roof of a one-room house. A wrinkled old codger greeted Hugh with a three-toothed smile and warmly invited him in for tea. Afterward the old man gave Hugh a tour of the local *gompa*. Hugh continued to poke around the gompa on his own while the man busied himself reciting verses and playing a drum. Three dimly lit walls were covered in faded frescoes. "Weird tantric stuff," Hugh noted in his journal. He left 5 rupees as a donation and when the man had finished his devotions they returned to his house for more tea.

"Where do you come from?" the man wanted to know.

"America," Hugh replied, expecting the old man to be amazed at the great distance he had traveled.

"Where?" the old man asked a second time.

"America," Hugh repeated.

"Amreekee? Never heard of the place!" came the response as the old man stirred the embers and brought the water to a boil. *Never even heard of America? This is amazing,* Hugh thought. The man made more tea as Hugh started to write in his diary,

> Here in Dett I was truly a long, lean stranger from a different universe. But a very real part of me felt as comfortable in these remote climes as I do in my own video-plagued town where the busiest place on a Saturday night is the parking lot at Blockbuster Video. It's not that I felt comfortable in Dett, but that I felt no less ill at ease than I do in my own country. For years I had laughed off my peculiar bicontinental shuffle of passing several months a year in the Himalayas by saying I was "over there." When I lived in the United States, I was "over here." But if I were traveling in the Himalayas, "over there" became "over here" and vice-versa. At any rate I was always over somewhere . . . never just "here." Now I realized I neither felt at home in Asia nor in the United States. Perhaps I had become trapped in a self-conscious nether world—a stranger no matter where I lived.

Before departing, Hugh gave the man a photo of the Dalai Lama, which he gladly accepted. The man referred to the Dalai Lama as Gyalpo Rimpoche, then touched the photograph to his forehead twice. Immersed in thoughts of a world where life was dictated by ancient traditions and the demands of the passing seasons, Hugh left Dett and wandered along the trail in search of Tashi. He realized he was as far from the values of his own culture as he would ever be, and during the afternoon walk he stopped frequently to write in his journal:

In Lahoul or Rupshu, I was considered outlandishly wealthy with my leather boots, expensive tent, and new umbrella. But in my own country, I'm thought a poor man who is wildly eccentric to boot, since I don't own a home or a car. I don't even have a checking account and I'm content to eat more or less the same meals, day in day out, a habit which wouldn't be given a second thought in Rupshu, where people have no choice.

When they broke camp the following morning, the air was noticeably colder and Tashi had switched to a knitted wool cap. They followed a deep gorge and soon came on four men, all dressed in maroon robes, who had set up a temporary altar with seven brass cups and a row of *torma* figures (molded pieces of tsampa mixed with water) decorated with thin pats of butter. A tremendous pile of sheep horns lay nearby, some carved with Tibetan

Dolpo region, Nepal.

inscriptions. One man brewed tea on a smoldering fire while the others chanted invocations to the protective deity Mahakala, the Great Black One, who was associated with a nearby sacred mountain. One man rang a bronze bell in the palm of his hand while a mass of weathered prayer flags rippled in the wind. During a break in the ceremony, they sipped salted and buttered tea and ate pinches of roasted barley flour. Taking in the scene, Hugh was once again moved by the depth to which these people had managed to integrate their everyday lives with their spiritual beliefs. A phenomenon virtually unknown in his own country.

At dinner that night Tashi asked about the printing on a plastic bread bag in which Hugh kept dry soup mix. It was an old bag but the price sticker was still legible: it read $2.19. Tashi was astonished when he converted the dollars to rupees. "Thirty-six rupees for less than a kilo of bread?" he exclaimed. Hugh told him that everything was expensive in America and that clothing, food, rent, and taxes consumed nearly all his money each year. "I live in a very cheap apartment, but I have to pay the equivalent of 8,000 rupees each month." This was more than Tashi spent in a year to feed his family and send his children to school.

The 16,000-foot-high rolling plains of Nimaling are known as "the meadows of sun," but days later, after a stiff two-hour climb, Hugh found the place bitterly cold, and teeming with marmots. The grazing was so bad at this time of the year that Tashi had taken the precaution to bring extra grass from their last camp so that the horses would have something to eat. Beyond the herds of cows, sheep, goats, horses, and donkeys that dotted the plains of Nimaling, Hugh spotted three nylon tents—a sure sign they were approaching the end of the journey. After three weeks on the trail, it was a shock to see these first traces of "civilization." For many travelers, Hemis Gompa is an ultimate destination in Ladakh, but for Hugh and Tashi the monastery marked the end of their journey and heralded a return to the world of roads and villages.

At their final camp Hugh continued to reflect on Tashi's skills as a guide and friend, and what different lives Tashi's sons would lead. Hugh remembered the older boy slicking his hair in front of the mirror and the younger son dreaming of becoming a jet pilot. When Tashi was a young man, six different dialects had been spoken in Lahoul district, but with the building of the road near Jispa Hindi had become the common language for government, business, and education. To better assimilate with the other students, his daughter Tsering had taken the name Bimla Devi for the Hindu school she attended. And, what would he do if the dam was constructed? He knew his sons would soon move away from Jispa in search of work, and in the span of a few years Tashi had witnessed the beginning of the end of the family farm and the rural community that he had been brought up in.

The electricity that the government was promising would do him little good if his home and fields were submerged by the new dam.

For their final breakfast of the journey, Tashi went to the extra effort of cooking *parathas*—flaky rounds of flatbread. They packed the horses and got off to a leisurely start. As they crested the summit of Kangmaru La, the last pass, a brief snow flurry dusted the ground. From the pass they overlooked the Indus Valley, where six thousand feet below them, obscured by a cloud bank, lay Hemis Gompa and the end of the journey. As a sign of the changing seasons, shepherds and their animals were already moving down the distant mountainsides as Hugh and Tashi followed a steep trail that zig-zagged down a ravine filled with rock rubble. Within hours of leaving the pass, they could feel the first heat of the valley, and by late morning the trail had leveled out and they were walking

OPPOSITE **Rangdum monastery, Zanskar, Ladakh.**

through a green valley bordered by purple scree slopes.

Poplar trees, vegetable gardens, and apricot orchards appeared, and by the whitewashed, flat-roofed buildings of Hemis Gompa Hugh said goodbye to Tashi. He paid him for the journey and then placed a *kata* (prayer scarf) around his neck for good luck and a safe journey home. The little man handed Hugh an apple that he had carried from Jispa, then headed back into the mountains, leaving Hugh with memories of the simple, uncomplicated times that he had shared with Tashi and his two horses, Bara and Chota.

The night Hugh told me this story, I walked to the wall of his apartment where the portrait of Tashi hung. I examined the photo, carefully taking in the details of his clothing, the expression on his face, and the landscape in the background. During my infrequent visits to the apartment, I always checked to see that Tashi's picture was where I remembered it. As for the other portraits, who knows where these men came from or what thoughts they stimulated in Hugh when he looked at them? These pictures represented trips to places we will never know about, but for Hugh they must have evoked memories of friendships and the thrill of strange encounters in remote places. For the rest of us, the portraits are just pictures of unknown people carefully stored in a cardboard box. They have been reduced to mementos. Indecipherable, precious, and irreplaceable. Whoever those men are, their portraits, like Hugh's, represent a lifetime of travel into a world that is rapidly changing forever.

4

BIG MOUNTAINS,
HAPPY PEOPLE
THE CHANGING FACE
OF SHANGRI-LA

Part of the middle-class tragedy
lies in the facility with
which intense experience can
be synthesized and bought.

MORITZ TOMSEN,
THE SADDEST PLEASURE

We destroy the places we love.

HUGH SWIFT

TRAVELERS were different when Hugh set out on his first walk in the Himalayas. It was hard work getting to Nepal in the mid-1960s. Agonizingly slow, in most cases, and it took a considerable investment of time and effort to get there. The bonus was that most travelers were acculturated by the time they reached their destinations. Now it is possible to be in Kathmandu within twenty-four hours of leaving home, and most people arrive jet-lagged and in a state of culture shock. The great beauty and timeless quality of life in the Himalayas is what continues to draw visitors, yet as curious strangers our increasing numbers are diminishing the very things we are searching for. In our eagerness to capture experience it is important to tread lightly because the elusive, otherworldly magic that still exists in remote places can disappear like the mountain mist.

Many first-time visitors to the Himalayas assume that the remote villages are economically, socially, and environmentally frozen in time. This is hardly the case. Landscapes and cultures are in a state of change, as they always have been since the beginning of geologic time and human habitation. The difference now is that the Himalayan countries, especially Nepal, are rapidly embracing a Western subculture based on consumerism. The ancient trade routes (used by yak and donkey caravans) that have joined India and Tibet through the high passes of the Himalayas for hundreds of years are becoming less important as are the traditional items of trade: salt, tea, and Tibetan sheep wool. Hinduism and Tibetan Buddhism are both threatened by the lure of modern living. Commercial tourism, roads, foreign aid, and resource development projects are the main forces responsible for the change now taking place. We call this progress, but on the village level the sudden introduction of money and modern technologies is bringing social

OPPOSITE **Wool traders' camp, Dolpo.**

60

disruption to traditional communities that are based on a delicate balance of barter trade, pastoralism, and subsistence farming.

This is not to say that the local people have not had an impact on their own environment. Over generations, entire lowland mountain ranges have been terraced and irrigated for agriculture. Poorly regulated logging and the increasing need for firewood due to growing population has led to deforestation and habitat destruction over vast areas of Nepal and Northern India. Erosion and silting of streams are but two of many related problems created by what is known as the Third World energy crisis—the lack of firewood for fuel.

Visitors to Nepal often talk about the subtleties of cultural change in the remote border regions, but longtime foreign residents of Kathmandu, when questioned about environmental degradation, are much more inclined to discuss respiratory

OPPOSITE **Kali Gandaki Valley, Nepal.**

illnesses attributed to the blanket of smog that has filled Kathmandu Valley over the last ten years.

Visitors to Kathmandu in the early 1970s might have noticed an old storyteller who used to sit in front of a votive shrine not far from the Ganesh Temple in Durbar Square. During the winter months he would come to the same spot each night to retell the 2,000-year-old Hindu epic, the Ramayana. The first night I happened on the storyteller, he was seated waist deep in marigolds and surrounded on three sides by a large group of listeners, mainly women and children. The scene was illuminated by a single electric bulb of low wattage that glimmered from the overhead darkness. Accompanied by a harmonium, the storyteller sang out the intricate details of how Lord Ram had rescued his loyal wife Sita from the demon god Ravana. The crisp night air held the sweet fragrance of sandalwood incense as the seated audience responded with choral refrains to every

Sadhu with Michael Jackson T-shirt, Nepal.

nuance of the story. The man spoke Nepali, which I didn't understand, but from his mimicry I could tell he had reached the part of the story where Hanuman, the monkey general, was mobilizing the monkey army to build a land bridge from South India to the island of Sri Lanka, where Ram's wife Sita was being held. Every night for four months the man came to tell the story and each night the garlands of marigolds increased. The following year he returned to the same place to tell the story again. The emphasis was slightly different each year, because, like all good stories, it can be told in an endless number of ways.

Now most of the storytellers are gone from the side streets surrounding Durbar Square, and the best way to hear the Hindu epic, especially on cold winter nights, is by going to one of the many video shops and renting an Indian-made soap opera version for the evening. Signs of change are everywhere. Hugh once sighted a *sadhu* (Hindu ascetic) wearing a Michael

Jackson T-shirt and drinking Pepsi Cola. The Dalai Lama has appeared on the cover of French *Vogue,* reggae is often played at Nepali weddings in Kathmandu, and prayer wheels are being constructed from recycled milk cans. Croissants and cappuccino are available. Cappuccino in Kathmandu? It sounds as incongruous as salted yak butter tea in the Hamptons.

Twenty-five years ago, there were no trekking maps or guidebooks to speak of. To go on a walk, you just took a local bus to the trail head and started walking north up the biggest river valley in sight. At night you would eat and sleep with a local family. In 1971 I began a 300-mile walk into the Himalayas with $100 worth of rupees in small bills, a $3 pair of Chinese high-topped canvas shoes, a down sleeping bag, and the command of two Nepali phrases: "Do you have a place to sleep?" and "Do you have any food?" It is still possible to trek like this, but with a vast selection of hiking equipment to choose from at home and the proliferation of guest houses with view restaurants serving Western-style food all along the major trekking routes, how many are willing to stay with a local family and eat *dal bhat* for dinner?

Hugh once mentioned that the Himalayan trekking world was badly in need of a philosophy similar to the "clean climbing" ethic adopted by rock climbers many years ago. At the very least, trekking companies should provide their clients with detailed cultural guidelines of where they are going and, at the same time, resist the temptation of visiting sacred sites or fragile communities where tourism is inappropriate.

Mt. Kailas, "Crown Chakra of the World," "Precious Jewel of Glacial Snow," is located in the far west of Tibet. As Hugh wrote in his guide book to Nepal, West Tibet, and Bhutan, "Kailas is the most sacred mountain on Earth to the world's 800 million Hindus as well as Jains, Tibetan Buddhists, and Bon Pos." Home to both Shiva and Parvati and to the Tibetan guardian deity Demchog and his consort Dorje Phagmo, Mt. Kailas is one

ABOVE Tibetan pilgrim, Mt. Kailas.
OPPOSITE The South Face of Mt. Kailas, Tibet.

of many remote destinations that recently has been opened to commercial trekking. Traditional pilgrims express their devotion by circumambulating the mountain while performing full prostrations, known as *gyang chatsel*. The thirty-two-mile circuit of Mt. Kailas, using the full prostration method, can take two or three weeks. Until the mid-1980s, Mt. Kailas was one of the ultimate destinations for solo Western travelers. Now the pilgrimage is offered in glossy, mail-order catalogues that tempt "leading edge" group travelers to experience the sacred mountain not with mantras, prostrations, or hand-held prayer wheels but with video cameras and Goretex day packs filled with energy bars, electrolyte balancers, and toilet paper. What is happening at Mt. Kailas is characteristic of what is taking place throughout the Himalayas.

In a few isolated cases, the influx of foreign visitors has had a positive effect on the local economy. For example, when China closed the trade routes into Tibet in

1959, the Sherpa villagers of the Solo Khumbu region were able to find work with climbing groups drawn to the Everest region. The Sherpas excel as high-altitude porters. Many of them died climbing, but today they are at the forefront of the trekking business. As a Buddhist minority in a Hindu country they have realized direct economic benefits from visitors. The Kali Gandaki gorge and the Annapurna Sanctuary near Pokhara are two other areas where local innkeepers and porters have made a livelihood from the estimated 35,000 trekkers that visit the region each year. In most other areas, the life of the average villager has changed very little. They have their pictures taken hundreds of times by passing strangers and if they are lucky they can pick up work as porters, but substantial or long-term benefits from the fifty million tourist dollars that enter the country each year have yet to reach these people.

The arrival of large numbers of affluent Western visitors has left its mark. Garbage is the most visible evidence of unwitting trekkers, but their ignorance or disregard of local customs has also had a negative effect. One of Hugh's photos captioned, "Near *mani* wall do no toilet" sums up this problem. *Mani* walls are holy sites constructed of stones. The structures are commissioned by individuals to acquire good merit or as an expression of faith. Each stone is carved in low relief with the prayer *Om mani padme hum,* "I salute the jewel in the lotus." The image of a Western trekker fouling these religious sites with toilet paper, urine, and feces is no less outrageous than the sight of a person squatting between the pews of a church to perform the same function. But such behavior is not uncommon, and Hugh had a difficult time dealing with his inner conflict of bringing visitors to pristine villages and then writing guidebooks that would draw thousands more to the places he loved. The high end of the travel industry has refined itself to the point where trips are highly specialized, but regardless of whether the groups set forth as "spiritual tourists," "adventure travelers," "eco-tourists," or "special interest travelers," they all look and act the same to the local villagers. A Nepali farmer, who had known Hugh for years, once stopped him as he was leading a group around Annapurna, and asked, "Why do you keep bringing these fools with their cameras to our village?" It was a question to which Hugh was unable to give a convincing answer. One of the great ironies of Hugh's guide work was that as a group leader who had valuable insights into both worlds, he ended up spending a considerable amount of his time protecting the clients by keeping them in their cultural cocoons for the duration of the trip.

Nepal is a poor country, and one of the few ways to accumulate foreign exchange is to bring in more visitors. The present figure is about 250,000 per year, and the hope is to increase that number to one million by the year 2000. Less than 25 percent of these visitors are trekkers. Most of them

Near mani, do no toilet.

belong to tour groups that stay in hotels. It is true that the trekking and expedition industry has created jobs in rural areas for innkeepers, porters, and guides, and that a substantial portion of the small-scale equipment and trekking businesses are privately owned by Nepalis, but the big profits from tourism are made by the hotel owners in Kathmandu and the overseas booking agents.

The immediate problem of increasing the number of visitors by a factor of four is the strain it will put on the local water supply. Each new high-rise hotel (meaning fifty rooms in five or six stories) offers Western-style bathrooms; not including showers, it takes a considerable amount of water to flush each toilet three or four times a day. One flush represents a village family's water usage for at least one meal, maybe two. The benefits of this sort of tourist development are not distributed. For the nearby villagers, it simply means less water. If you travel to Kirtipur, a little town situated on a ridge behind the Trib-

huvan University, in Kathmandu Valley, you will notice the expanse of water jugs and urns all lined up and ready for that one hour a day when the village water tap gets turned on. When the time comes, everyone quickly fills up because it will be twenty-four hours before the water begins to flow again.

As part of the government program to generate more money from tourism, the decision was made to open up the restricted areas such as Humla, Mugu, Dolpo, Mustang, and Nupri. These areas represent the most delicate regions in the country both culturally and economically. And so, of course, everyone wants to be the first to go to these places. Lho Man-thang, the ancient and forbidden walled city of Mustang, is probably the most coveted destination in the country, and so after lengthy discussion with local residents the government decided to issue 500 individual permits per year. The cost of each permit was $700. The exclusive nature of such a journey proved irresistible, and so many people fronted up with the money that this year the quota was "limited" to 1,000. Who knows how many permits will be issued next year, or how much more some people might be willing to pay to visit Mustang?

When groups go into the formerly restricted areas, the first things that are up for grabs are the cultural artifacts. Many of the beautiful *thangkas,* statues, religious texts, even carved door and window frames—whatever can be lifted and carried—will disappear. This has happened throughout the rest of Nepal, and it will happen in Dolpo, Mustang, and everywhere else. Precious objects have a remarkably short shelf life once the gates are opened. Dealers, dishonest villagers, and wealthy collectors on the scent of historical art treasures make a formidable team that is in the process of stripping irreplaceable cultural artifacts from the region. Fifty-yak caravans have already carried away entire monasteries to storerooms in the United States. Not even

Temple horns, Bhutan.

human remains are safe from these individuals.

Many people, especially those in the business, would have us believe the relationship between trekkers and the locals is benign. But, as any experienced guide will tell you, there is more to the equation than mutual curiosity. Tour groups provide companionship and the possibility of romance and make it possible for people with money and limited time to visit remote locations. This is an extremely valuable and important service, but one cannot help realizing that there is going to be a huge impact when a dozen or so clients and their leader come into a mountain village with thirty-five porters and then proceed to set up camp. The trekkers are frequently wearing fashionable, multicolored clothing made from space-age fabrics and their feet are encased in priceless hiking boots. Then, like magicians' hats, the duffel bags are opened and out come these amazing tents, tables, and folding chairs, which are soon occupied by strangers from another

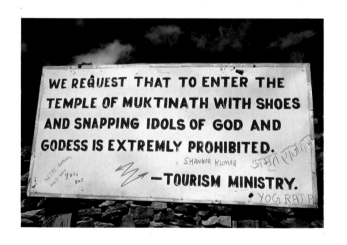

Muktinath, Annapurna, Nepal.

world. One of the early groups going into the remote Dolpo region brought along a "white noise" generator to block out the natural sounds of the mountains.

The Sherpa guides stand somewhere between the clients and the locals in terms of their diet, clothing, and behavior, and frictions between the Sherpas and the local community often simmer just below the surface. The clients rarely speak a word of Nepali, yet even with everyone just staring at one another, the Sherpa trek leaders can create problems without the members knowing anything is up. A problem can develop from the Sherpas chasing the local girls, playing at being heroes in front of the young boys, by flashing around in their expensive trekking clothes, spending large sums of money, getting stinking drunk, or buying up scarce commodities and food.

The natural thing for young boys in the village is to think, "Why am I standing around slapping dung patties on the wall or studying in school? I want to be one of these guys." And so the village boys start coming around the camp asking if they can work as porters. Then they hit the trail, and the trail always leads back to Kathmandu, and once they've been to Kathmandu they don't want to go home and work in the fields and haul water and cut firewood or end up marrying the poor girl from the next village. They want sunglasses and cowboy boots, leather jackets and Bob Marley tapes. By the early 1970s these displaced villagers had become so numerous on New Road in Kathmandu that even the Nepalis referred to them as "New Road Cowboys." This dynamic will continue with the opening up of the remote areas along the Tibetan border.

Individual trekkers with local knowledge or language skills have always managed to wander into every corner of the country, but their impact has been negligible. The standard technique for travel into restricted areas was to forge a trekking permit and grease a few palms to get past the police checkposts on the trail.

Groups, on the other hand, were originally restricted to the standard routes like Solo Khumbu, Langtang, the Kali Gandaki, and Annapurna Sanctuary as well as a few other places, but now, as the remaining areas open up, the cultural impact spreads at a greater rate. Evidence of this process is easily observed on the standard trekking routes. *Mani Rimdu,* the Tibetan dance drama held each year at Tengboche monastery, is still one of the most important religious festivals of the region, but after fifteen years of growing Western audiences unfamiliar with the language, music, costumes, or plot, many Sherpas now consider the performance to be more of a tourist attraction than a spiritual or religious event.

Social values everywhere are in a perpetual state of change, but what is happening in the rural areas of Nepal is that the natural rate of change is being accelerated to the point where there is little time for people to digest or absorb new ideas. It is a case of "adapt as best you can and get a share of the profits" because there will be no going back to how things were before.

Very little of this sort of change is being recorded by the stream of photojournalists passing through the Himalayas with their cameras, cartons of film, and magazine deadlines. They fire away with motor drives at the local people and landscapes, and the primary goal seems to be to stake out as much territory as possible and to perpetuate the myth of Shangri-La. A British photographer, while on assignment, wanted to abandon a porter who was deathly ill. His reasoning? "I can't wait," the photographer complained, "I'm on a deadline." The group finally halted and the man lived, but from that day on the porters referred to the photographer as "the hungry ghost." Hungry ghosts, well-known mythological figures depicted in the Tibetan "wheel of life" *thangkas,* are characterized by their insatiable quest for self-gratification. They will suck the life force out of anyone who stands in their way.

Thumbing through Hugh's archives one

day, I came upon an article from *Himal* magazine that told a similar story of abuse. In 1988 a young porter had died on the Thorong La, the 17,770-foot pass that links the upper Kali Gandaki gorge with the Marsyangdi Valley behind Annapurna. Without adequate footwear, mittens, or warm clothing, the porter was found frozen to death in a snow bank. He was dressed in a corduroy sport coat and a thin cotton shirt. The trekking party of the American couple that hired the man had evidently rummaged through his carrying basket, removed the items they needed and then thrown a lightweight sleeping bag over the body before continuing on their Himalayan adventure. The porter was found surrounded by onions, potato peelings, discarded packets of instant hot chocolate powder, and freeze-dried trekking food. His battered eating plate lay nearby. This was not an isolated incident, and looking at a photograph of the dead man I tried, without success, to imagine Hugh taking Tashi or one of his other

Kathmandu Valley, Nepal.

guides into the mountains without proper clothing or abandoning them if they fell ill or were suffering from frostbite. Poor lowland porters will carry well over 100 pounds for three or four dollars a day, yet there are foreign visitors who will leave them for dead if they can't keep up the pace.

Mountain-climbing expeditions have had a slightly different effect. I once followed a joint Japanese-Iranian expedition up the Buri Gandaki Valley to Manaslu in 1976 and witnessed how entire regions are pillaged for food and firewood. To get stuck behind one of these groups with their hundreds of porters and dozens of climbers is like following Sherman on his march to the sea. The only hope for relief rests in stepping up the pace and passing the group before the food supply runs out. When a big expedition comes through a village, food prices soar and it becomes a simple supply-and-demand situation. If travelers can't buy eggs, milk, or chickens because all sources of protein have been vacuumed up by the expedition, what are the children in the village eating? Children are deprived of this food because it is all being sold for cash, and this cash is probably not going for other food. In all likelihood it will be spent on a bottle of *arak* for Dad, or it will go toward the purchase of a new tape player.

Hugh never participated in a mountain-climbing expedition, and the very idea of risking his life or spending the time climbing to the top of a Himalayan peak seemed like utter nonsense to him. But he was familiar with these groups, and he once gave me an account of the British Blackspur Expedition to climb Makalu in 1989. The expedition was not the worst of its kind, by any means, but in many ways it typified what happens when large groups of people are moved into the backcountry. In telling the story, it never occurred to Hugh to mention whether the climbers reached the summit.

There were ten members on the

expedition plus two filmmakers, a still photographer, and a government liaison officer from Kathmandu. To support this number of climbers, there were over 120 porters going into base camp. The rules say that kerosene or bottled fuel must be used in high-altitude areas, but, as in most cases, the porters were not carrying kerosene and stoves with which to do their cooking. Instead, they cut green wood from a nearby rhododendron forest, and they cut a substantial amount of it because it was cold and they weren't properly provided with adequate bedding or clothing. Every ten porters cut a good five-foot-high stack of green wood to burn for the evening and for breakfast the next morning. After breakfast they went out and cut some more. The Blackspur Expedition was only one of seven expeditions in the fall of 1989. Then there was the spring climbing season, and Makalu is just one of dozens of major climbs attempted each year.

That same season there was a Spanish expedition camped above the British climbers. The Spanish members had signed an agreement with the Nepali government and Ministry of Tourism that they would only use liquid or bottled fuel, but once they arrived it wasn't long before the porters were down in the same rhododendron forest cutting wood and bringing it up to base camp at 18,000 feet so the climbers could barbecue pigs and chickens. It's not that the expedition wasn't using some bottled fuel, but at that altitude they were miserable and wanted to sit around a fire and warm their hands and feet and enjoy the comfort of a campfire. And who can blame them? They were up there for two to three months getting acclimatized and waiting for the perfect day for each stage of the climb. When you figure the number of these expeditions, the wood use is immense. Then there is the human waste and garbage problem. The base camp at nearby Mt. Everest has the highest-altitude dump on Earth. Sixteen tons (a small portion of the total) of the accumulated garbage and discarded expedition gear was removed by the Nepal police in 1984.

Over in the western part of Nepal, you don't find nearly as much moisture as in the Makalu region, and consequently there are no rhododendron forests near the prime climbing areas. Instead, one finds a scattering of ancient shrub alpine juniper on the hillsides. Some of these stunted trees take fifty to eighty years to mature, and many of them never reach maturity because they end up providing about ten or fifteen minutes' worth of firewood for a group of climbers who want to stand on top of the world for a few minutes and take pictures of each other.

The most cost-effective use of firewood that I know of was in the Sherpa village of Namche Bazaar, near Mt. Everest, during the winter of 1976. A local hotel owner had come up with the idea of providing hot showers for trekkers. After three or four weeks on the trail these people really wanted to take a proper shower, especially the Western women. Considering the tremendous amount of expensive wood required to heat the water, and the low price of a shower, it seemed like a marginal operation, but yet the man prospered. Only later was his secret revealed. The man was making huge profits by charging his friends to look through peek holes in the shower walls while naked white women soaped themselves up. Local interest flared, then faded, and competition from other hotel owners eventually exhausted the market. After that, shower prices soared, and the water was tepid.

Over the span of twenty-five years Hugh continued to document the different aspects of change taking place in the Himalayas. His notebooks are sprinkled with observations on travelers and mountain climbers, but in recent years he managed to expand his vision to take in the international army of foreign aid experts from organizations such as The World Bank, USAID (United States Agency for

International Development), and UNDP (United Nations Development Program). These people are known as the aid game players, and one of their specialties is to perpetuate the myth that aid will open up horizons for a new and improved quality of life. But the reality is that Nepal is a delicate and fragile land and with big egos, careers, and large sums of money being thrown around, it is usually change that takes place first—followed by someone trying to go back and study the situation and correct the mistakes or rewrite the original goals in order to match the results. The activities of these people added greatly to the bulk of Hugh's archives, and he occasionally came across their handiwork while on the trail.

Alongside the major aid game players are those who are commonly referred to as "chain letter researchers"—the ones who specialize in garnering grant and consultancy money in return for passing on the facts they have inherited. The primary purpose of the research is the presentation of material that becomes an integral part of the next proposal. You get yourself a budget to work on a project with the aim of building yourself into the continuation of that project. Ideally, you plug yourself into one of the well-funded agencies. But what is the end product? A ranch in Montana? A second wife in Southern California? A holiday home in Bali?

The popular mini hydroelectric projects illustrate what can result from the sudden introduction of Western technology. In one village, the plan was to install a mini hydro to help cut down the use of firewood. Once the mini hydro was built it was assumed the villagers would reduce their wood consumption because they could use electric lighting. But follow-up studies have shown that when people have electric lights at night they stay up later, and in order to stay warm they burn much more wood than before. This also affects their work habits because the people stay up late drinking alcohol and are less productive the next day. So the net result was

negative as far as wood consumption and productivity were concerned.

What the aid experts hadn't considered was that mini hydro plants also made it possible for a remote mountain village to operate a VCR. With a VCR, the back-pedaling aid workers reasoned, the villagers could watch educational tapes and learn how to reforest their hillsides or diversify their crops. As Hugh noted in his journal, this idea was about as successful as trying to market *The Life Cycle of Corn Bore Larvae* at Blockbuster Video, and it wasn't long before the villagers discovered much more interesting videos—like *Rambo, Hulk Hogan,* and triple-X-rated pornographic films from Bangkok. This sort of entertainment is now found in villages all the way up and down the Kali Gandaki Valley—one of the most scenic and popular trekking areas in Nepal.

In a more ambitious mini hydro project the American Himalayan Foundation,

OPPOSITE **Tengboche monastery, 1912–1988.**

based in San Francisco, came up with the idea of electrifying Tengboche monastery. Constructed in 1912, the monastery, one of the most beautiful and transporting buildings in the Himalayas, was situated on a spur just beneath the magnificent peak of Ama Dablam. The head lama was lukewarm about the idea, but members of the American Himalayan Foundation wanted a high-visibility project and managed to convince him of the benefits of electricity. It would help conserve firewood, they explained. The project, at a cost of approximately $100,000, was completed in 1988. The American VIP donors flew in by helicopter for the big opening ceremony. The switch was thrown, and within a year the place had burned to the ground because of an electrical fire.

One project that Hugh kept notes on came to fruition in the mid-1980s. It was called the Resource Conservation and Utilization Project, or RCUP. It included the regions of Baglam, Megbe, Mustang, Dolpo, and a few other districts below

Annapurna and Dhaulagiri. Large blue signboards were erected and painted with white letters and a big handshake—a sure indication from USAID that another joint Nepali/American development project was underway. As far as the conservation and use of resources was concerned, the project got as far as building a series of gigantic (by Nepali village standards) concrete structures in very remote areas. The primary purpose of these prestigious-looking buildings was to lure upper caste or Western-educated Nepali civil servants into accepting posts in isolated areas. What no one had considered, during the design phase of the project, was how to heat one of these structures. To do so, they would have had to consume—completely—the very wood resources they were trying to protect. Huge sums were spent to develop a basic infrastructure, but only limited aspects of the program were ever implemented. The empty buildings, however, still exist because they were constructed with yards and yards of concrete.

The final tally was 174 empty buildings at a cost of 27.5 million dollars.

Another aid project, also designed without consulting the local people, was a public toilet for the town of Patan in Kathmandu Valley. The plan was to build a communal toilet on a circular floor plan. People would squat in their little cubicles, and the excrement and urine would be collected into a central holding tank that was part of a methane gas digester. Then, the reasoning went, everyone could cook their food using the gas. Well, first of all, Newaris may use dried animal dung as fuel, but they are not going to cook their meals with gas produced from human excrement, especially excrement from different castes. The Newaris of Kathmandu Valley, like all Hindus, are very careful about how they prepare their food. It has to do with pollution, caste considerations, and ritual, and so one would be hard pressed to convince Newaris to cook their food in that way just because it may be efficient to use the gas from human excrement.

Even basic services, the sort that we take for granted, have received unexpected reactions. In the mid-1970s, Hugh Downs, author of *Rhythms of a Himalayan Village,* once asked a paper seller in Kathmandu what he thought about the new electrical service. "I don't like it," he said, "We used to have a vision of Shiva right up there (pointing to the sky) every week. The vision would walk down the street, and the shopkeepers would lay out offerings and burn incense. But once those power lines went up the vision never came back again." By local standards, the neighborhood had gone to hell.

Not all aid projects have turned into the fiascoes that seem to mark many of the efforts of the World Bank, UNDP, and USAID. While these three organizations are often detached from the basic human needs of villagers, there are other groups that specialize in community development. Unicef and Oxfam are frequently involved with children and education. Seva (a Sanskrit word for "service") operates fifteen

Winnowing barley, Dolpo region, Nepal.

Boy with marigold garland,
Tihaar Festival, Nepal.

eye centers throughout Nepal and has been instrumental in creating approximately fifty eye camps each year in rural areas. Seva staff perform cataract surgery and are dedicated to the prevention and cure of blindness at minimal cost. In a similar fashion, Peace Corps projects have provided drinking water systems, foot bridges, agricultural assistance, and math and science teachers. Female Peace Corps volunteers teach Nepali women about hygiene, prenatal care, and early childhood development.

Even privately funded projects with a special focus have succeeded. Not long after Tengboche monastery went up in flames a small group of Hugh Swift's friends, without any publicity, managed to completely rebuild a seventeenth-century Tibetan Buddhist monastery. The organizers recognized the importance of guarding the privacy of the monastery and, as a result, many of the patrons who donated generously have little sense of where the building is located.

"People have been part of the Himalayan ecosystem for a long time," explains Dr. J. Gabriel Campbell, director of the Woodlands Mountain Institute and Mt. Everest Ecosystem Conservation Program. "But it is only recently that large-scale changes have been introduced. These changes—roads, vehicles, new agricultural technologies, hydropower, and foreign visitors—open up new horizons for a better quality of life but also pose dangers to the ecosystem never faced before. Together, we're working to effectively manage all that."

This statement, typical of many aid organizations, gives the impression that development is under control and moving along nicely, according to some orderly plan. Government population figures present an entirely different picture of where the country is headed. Approximately 20 million people live in Nepal. The birth rate stands at about 2.6 percent, which means that the population will double in another twenty-five years. In a country where the per capita annual income is

around $150 and the resource base is crumbling, it should be fairly obvious that the quality of life is going to be driven down by the rapidly expanding population. Many of the rural Nepalese are aware of this problem, and when one village discovered that the local USAID worker was against funding population control (on the basis of Christian fundamentalism rather than cost), residents became concerned that USAID had fallen under the influence of some sort of kooky religious cultism.

The accumulated effect of five decades of foreign aid has led to a situation where expectations have been raised, but the people are just as poor as they were before. One of the ironies of foreign aid in Nepal is that, no matter how many millions of dollars are spent on a wide variety of programs, the big environmental problems of soil erosion, population, lack of land, and vanishing forests remain undiminished. In some cases the problems seem to be getting worse. For example, despite the substantial efforts of organizations such as the Nepal-Australia Forestry Project in the Sindhu Palchok and Kabhre districts of central Nepal, half of the country's forest has vanished since the 1950s.

Tony Hagen, a geologist and aid consultant from Switzerland, helped introduce Nepal to the world in the 1950s and has watched the aid game since the beginning. He uses the term *Mittelabflusswang,* which is an expression in the development vocabulary. It refers to the need to disburse, or get rid of, aid money. And with donor countries throwing money at Nepal with little coordination or planning or follow-up studies, why shouldn't the aid takers accept the money? One of the biggest problems he has observed is the tendency of aid managers to fund only the most visible, expensive, and prestigious projects. Environmental objectives are swept aside by local politics and (in his words) by "the shortsighted and ruthless consumer needs of the industrialized countries and Third World elites."

And what is more impressive than a mighty dam? Ever since the beginning of modernization in 1951, the Nepalis have been mesmerized with the thought of developing their hydroelectric potential and growing rich by selling the power to the energy-starved industrialized northern regions of India. The most recent in a series of projects that are aimed at realizing this dream is located on the upper Arun River. The mammoth project is known as Arun III. The World Bank is planning to finance the project, which is budgeted in the billions of dollars. The goal, as described by Prime Minister Krishna Prasad Bhattarai in Kathmandu in October 1990, is to solve the trade deficit problem with India, and everyone seems to be stupefied by the prospect of all those potential hydro-dollars. The proposed hydro facility at the junction of the Arun and Barun rivers will require a very sizable access road to bring in heavy equipment necessary to bore a tunnel and bisect an oxbow in the river. The diversion of water through the tunnel will create the hydraulic head with which to generate power. A sizable diversion dam is also planned. No one is certain what might happen during the monsoon season, and with the possibility of earthquakes, landslides, and erosion from the deforested hillsides, it is questionable how long the three-billion-dollar project will be viable if the dam silts up. People have suggested a series of smaller "run of the river" hydro projects in a variety of locations so that all the eggs aren't in one basket, but in the meantime the World Bank has purchased all the land needed for the access road.

When Hugh asked the resettlement expert for the World Bank (who has done extensive fieldwork in Nepal and has a doctorate in anthropology) if there was some plan or educational project to explain to the villagers about the repercussions of the road or how to reinvest the money or make a living without land, the expert replied, "Oh, what an interesting idea." This man was in charge of not only Nepal but everywhere else in the world where big projects and loan opportunities require the displacement of people.

Supporters of the Arun III project claim that the dam will bring diversity of livelihood, when in fact the sole purpose of the project is to sell electricity to India in order to balance the trade deficit because so many goods are imported from India. The relocation scheme is merely an exercise in moving people for profits.

Governments and businessmen in Third World countries have always been willing to play the aid game, mainly for profit and power. When the aid money starts to reach your knees, it becomes very difficult to resist reaching down to grab some of it. Rhetoric has been modernized, but this sort of aid is really modeled after the colonial system that expedites the removal of natural resources while promising the benefits of salvation or development. In Nepal's case, the potential wealth lies in hydroelectric power, timber, and tourism. As far as diversity of livelihood and higher standards of living are concerned, little if anything has happened.

Searching through the archives, it came as a relief to finally uncover the story of a project that didn't adhere to this formulaic, profit-driven approach to aid. An agricultural team had come from Japan to help increase yields and diversify crops in Kathmandu Valley. The Japanese were good listeners, and after thoroughly researching what was being done and conducting intensive interviews with the Newari Japu farmers of the valley, the Japanese experts concluded that they had nothing to teach the farmers about irrigation, crop rotation, soil nutrients, or marketing. In fact, by listening and watching, the Japanese learned a great deal and made the uncommonly wise decision not to meddle with a system that already worked.

After nearly fifty years of change brought about by foreign aid, politics, resource development, and tourism, the Himalayan kingdom of Nepal finally dissolved in riots and gunfire during the pro-democracy demonstrations in the spring of 1990. At the time of the uprising, people discovered that by removing the front of their radios and advancing the tuning dial it was possible to pick up the police and army radio band and listen to orders being exchanged between field commanders and their troops. A friend of Hugh's, listening to the radio during the riots in Kathmandu, related what he heard as an army officer and his men faced a crowd of demonstrators:

"They are coming now . . . form a line." There was a pause, followed by, "They are coming . . . fire warning shots." A few shots are heard, then, "They are still coming . . . they are still coming! Fire at their legs [crackle of gunfire]." Static interrupted the transmission, but before the reception faded he could hear the commander shouting, "They are still coming, hold the line . . . SHOOT TO KILL, SHOOT TO KILL!"

In the span of fifty years, the medieval kingdom of Nepal had joined the modern world.

5

BESIDE THE
PERFUMED RIVER

*In the end our endeavours
were themselves our reward.*

SHEPPARD CRAIGE

WHEN HUGH was a child, his family often drove from Pennsylvania to Colorado to visit his grandparents during the summer. At the conclusion of one of these trips, Hugh took a pair of scissors to his father's road maps. He cut out the states they had driven through, Scotch-taped them together in proper sequence, and then marked the route in crayon. He pinned the maps to the ceiling of his bedroom with thumb tacks so that he could daydream about the trip while lying in bed. As he grew up, the only thing that changed was the scale of those maps and his capacity for details. A friend recently remarked that Hugh's inner world was an incredibly detailed map of the Himalayas—a topographic reality that occupied the limits of his spatial imagination.

When he grew older, Hugh—as pilgrim, consummate outsider, and curious stranger—felt compelled to return again and again to places from his past. The sites of his pilgrimages were diverse and well scattered. They ranged from the Times Square Record Shop and the Apollo Theater in Manhattan, to the bathing ghats of Benares, the Kumba Mela festival in Allahabad, Amarnath Cave in Kashmir (where he ran his hand over Shiva's frozen lingam), to holy Mt. Kailas, and finally back to Vietnam, where he had once taught English at Quac Hoc High School in Hue.

Hugh had a need to reconnect periodically with the people and places from his past, and perhaps it was from this need that he finally returned to Hue, the ancient Imperial City of Vietnam, and to the banks of the Song Huong—the Perfumed River. Hugh had left Hue shortly before the Tet offensive in 1968, and on his return to the city, with a group of former IVS volunteers, the first thing he noticed was that much of the Dai Noi (the Citadel), scene of vicious hand-to-hand fighting and mortar and aerial bombardments, had been planted in vegetable

OPPOSITE **Indian pilgrimage, Mt. Kailas.**

ABOVE **Nomad, West Tibet.**
OPPOSITE **Dolma Pass, Mt. Kailas.**

gardens. The lush vegetation must have flourished on the nutrient-rich soil that resulted from the human carnage.

One morning, as the mist was still rising from the river, Hugh, lost in recollections of a former self, wandered through Hue searching for landmarks from his past: the high school, the house where he once lived, and the familiar marketplaces. The merchandise of one street vendor caught his eye. It was limited to a small woven tray filled with firecrackers and condoms. While Hugh was walking through the old neighborhoods and along the Perfumed River, the rest of his group went on a river cruise. During the tour one of the group asked their Vietnamese guide where he had learned English.

"From a tall American . . . Mr. Swift," the guide replied.

"Hugh Swift?" someone exclaimed, quite certain they had not heard the man correctly.

Marilyn Young, one of the group members, described what happened next: "We

Ngozumpa glacier and Gokya Lake, Nepal.

told the guide that Hugh was on the trip, though we didn't know where he was at the moment, and he got incredibly excited. He would have dove off the boat if possible. We landed and went on to the Citadel and there, in the shadow of the great archway leading into its central plaza, we could see Hugh's tall form. Our guide saw him a moment after we did and he began to walk, then half-run towards him. Hugh heard a commotion, turned, saw, all unbelieving at first, who it was and then they hugely embraced, there in the gateway, all the years and the deaths falling away. And those of us who saw what was happening wept."

The guide was Thuan—the young Vietnamese student who had taken Hugh home in 1965 and introduced him to his family, to Southeast Asia—and to a way of being that changed him for life. Hugh had thought about the family for twenty-five years, and he often wondered what had become of them. He had been especially fond of Thuan's mother and had carried the memory of her hospitality and kindness for all those years. When he mentioned her name, Thuan told him that she had been killed by artillery fire in the 1968 Tet offensive—two weeks after Hugh had left the city.

When Hugh died in 1991, he was working on a collection of stories he referred to as the Himalayan Patchwork. In a handwritten rough draft of a book proposal he wrote down his thoughts on photography, writing, travel, and life.

"Photography has a funny way of distancing you from your subject. You often have to be elsewhere taking pictures when the light is right, rather than eating with the family you are visiting. . . . Some photographers are as culturally sensitive as mountaineers, perhaps even less so. They stand apart from the people they 'shoot,' seeing them as subjects, not as people. There is no rapport—only questions of composition, focus, depth of field, and light." Looking at Hugh's photos, one never gets the sense that he was the interloper or intrusive observer with money or prestige on his mind. Hugh's sensitivity to the people, his language skills, sense of humor, and twenty-five-year association with the Himalayas put him in a category of his own. Friendship always came first, and this approach produced a unique collection of warm and personal photographic images. One got the sense that he was taking pictures of his friends or of his neighborhood, and in a way he was doing just that. So vast was his knowledge of people and places, of where to go, when, and how—that even NBC and *National Geographic* would consult Hugh before sending journalists to remote areas in the Himalayas.

In the margin of his book proposal, he scribbled, "The whole process [of being published] changed me and in some ways it distanced me from my experience of the hills. Now when I go into the mountains there is a burden placed on me to observe, take notes, and get that photo. I find myself wondering how someone can help me with what I'm doing, rather than just enjoying that person, and it doesn't feel right."

One aspect of our society that irritated Hugh greatly was the average American's near-perfect ignorance of the rest of the world. This attitude grew out of Hugh's experience in Vietnam and his travels in Asia where he learned to delight in the company of strangers. For many Western-ers, he realized, Europe represented the outer limits of civilization, while other countries, conveniently grouped under the heading of "The Third World," might as well be located on Planet X for all that was known about them. Part of Hugh's desire to take photographs and write about his journeys was to illuminate those "other places"—the hidden corners. Having trav-eled and worked for nearly twenty years in Asia, North Africa, the Middle East, and Southeast Asia, I can well appreciate Hugh's quest for the everyday hospitality, generosity of spirit, and kindness that seem to have been bred out of our society.

Yak caravan, Gujal area, Northern Pakistan.

Hugh was best known for the obscure places he visited and the number of miles he walked, but I am certain that it was the contact with local people that drew him back to the Himalayas over and over again.

Hugh never fully came to terms with leading groups into the Himalayas, or marketing his vast knowledge of the area. He was taking part in a cultural invasion and realized that by divulging remote trails and bringing people to the places he loved that he was contributing to the end of those places as he had known them. Hugh's comment "We kill the places we love" revealed his growing discomfort with how he made a living, and the dilemmas he faced by exposing too much about what he knew best.

Hugh was much more settled about the nature of his solo journeys. Shortly before his death he wrote, "Travel consumes me. My 'real life' at home in America is put aside completely for the months I am away. The thought of reflecting on American life while traveling is not possible [and]

Near Mt. Kailas, Tibet.

perhaps my sojourns in the USA are just periods of treading water until I again return to the far more intensely lived stage of Asia, where I can again become the consummate outsider . . . the curious stranger."

Reflecting on other accounts of travel in the Himalayas, Hugh wrote, "Some books appear with white-knuckled tales of abandonment by locals, swollen rivers, robberies and such, but the people who experienced these misadventures often incurred them because they made inept mistakes themselves. If my travels don't have enough treachery or cliff-hanging situations, it is because I have tried to go places at the right season with the right people and have endeavored to make a

friend, not a pest out of myself with the people I've met."

Hugh was best known for his lack of pretense, his generosity, simplicity, friendship, and love of the odd and unusual. It seems ironic that after a lifetime of trying to understand and integrate with a world that was not his own, the only written feedback he ever received from his guidebooks was from a disgruntled reader who wrote from India, saying he wanted his money back.

One of Hugh's last journal entries reads, "Make your own myth, your own fable, don't live by others'." It was an ideal that Hugh chose to live by—a vision he kept faith with until the end.

OPPOSITE **Walking the Annapurna massif, Nepal.**

A NOTE ABOUT THE PHOTOGRAPHS

Hugh worked primarily with one camera and one lens. Through the worn edges and corners of Hugh's trusty old black-bodied Nikon shone the golden brass, a testament to the wear and tear on the camera. Carrying a tripod and large arsenal of lenses, filters, backup camera bodies, and accessories was not Hugh's style. Details about the focal length of Hugh's lenses or the f-stops and shutter speeds at which he recorded his travels would tell little about Hugh the photographer. It is more useful to know that the camera was as essential to Hugh as his umbrella. And like the umbrella, Hugh's camera served him everywhere. Through his photographs, Hugh puts us on the trail, at the top of the pass, or in dialogue with his Balti buttermakers, Sherpa lamas, and Ladakhi porters. His most memorable images blend the particulars of places and people with his own warmth and easygoing personal style. The results give us a comfortable sense of familiarity with even the wildest and most exotic subject matter. Hugh's careful process of collecting data and recording the visual facts of a place is balanced with whimsy, silliness, and a boundless appreciation for visual incongruities.

A vast array of equipment choices and the compulsion to endlessly motor-drive rolls of chrome film through the camera ensure that professional photographers meet their deadlines and usually overshoot their stories. Hugh did not work hastily under the constraint of deadlines, but rather with a concern to slowly, over the years, build an archive of slides of the entire Himalayan region. His collection of slides was both a stock library and an extension of Hugh's idiosyncratic sensibilities.

Along with camels being shod in Tajikistan one finds the guns-and-drugs market of Peshawar in Pakistan, the funkiest footbridges and the funniest signboards of the Himalaya, and portraits of Kathmandu Valley's most extraordinary expatriates. Cumulatively, the images are Hugh's "Himalayan patchwork." His photos are not all perfect exposures or perfect compositions, where everything is neatly and comfortably packed in the frame, but each one imparts Hugh's warmth and his quirky and endearing vision.

There was a quiet, considerate deliberateness to Hugh's way of photographing. The tedious procedure of bringing the camera out of his day-pack or the folds of his down coat, then releasing his eyeglasses from one ear so that they dangled from the other ear, ensured that Hugh's images were never quickly captured. After each exposure, the film in the old Nikon was thoughtfully advanced to the next frame while Hugh repositioned his eyeglasses, surveyed, and reevaluated the subject or scene in front of him. This was Hugh's ritual.

Simplicity and compactness were essential not only to Hugh's photographic gear but to his note-taking, journal keeping, and slide captioning as well. Hugh's printing was so minuscule that his line-a-day journal entries for an entire two-month journey would cover only one sheet of letter paper. These notations were the framework on which he constructed expanded journal writings and slide captions.

Over time, much of Hugh's photography documenting places revealed the breadth of change in the Himalayan landscape. This was particularly true of the Annapurna circuit, Khumbu,

and the Kathmandu Valley—three places Hugh photographed repeatedly. None of the changing scene escaped Hugh's scrutiny. His images show previously untouched trails sprouting new trekking lodges and signboards, Kathmandu's traditional clay tile rooftops being decked with satellite dishes, and Khumbu's Sherpas sporting the latest in outdoor wear.

The vastness of the territory Hugh covered and the extent of his subject matter only really struck me when Eric Hansen asked me to join the book team as photoeditor in June of 1992. In the photos I found Tibetan guide Karma Chumbey with Hugh's frequent trekking companion, Chris Wriggins, on their way up the Humla Karnali River in 1974. Karma Chumbey also appears in Hugh's photos of at least four successive treks in northwestern Nepal over the next eighteen years. We see Hugh's friend John Mock dancing to the drums and flutes of a northern Pakistani border police band, and then with Hugh on Nepal's Mustang Dolpo border several years later. Back in Kathmandu, Ted Wooster looks the perfect Santa Claus, throwing penny candy to a large flock of Tibetan and expatriate children. Then, aboard his BMW motorcycle, he is enroute to the Bouddhanath *stupa* to share Christmas cheer.

In September of 1992 I arrived at Eric Hansen's house in Sacramento where six large cardboard cartons of Hugh's slides awaited me. These were Hugh's images from twenty-five years of travel. Each carton held eight three-ring binders filled with thirty to forty slide sheets. Most of the slides from the last two years had been sleeved into sheets without any notation or even Hugh's rubber copyright stamp on them. In all, there were nearly fifteen thousand slides to be edited down to a manageable number for this book.

I felt humbled by the responsibility of editing Hugh's slides. While I could gauge the relative strength of the transparencies according to aesthetic and technical standards, my friend was no longer there to answer questions about his photographs. I could only guess at the stories the images would trigger in Hugh if he had been there to tell them.

Traveling vicariously with Hugh through the slides spread before me on the light table, I was struck enormously by the jagged landscapes of northern Pakistan and Zanskar and the austerity of the Chiangtang plateau of Tibet. It would be hard for anyone who knows the Himalayan region not to marvel at the geographical breadth of Hugh's photographic archive. While there would be slides of familiar places, there undoubtedly would be numerous new discoveries for even the most seasoned Himalayan traveler.

Somewhere between slide pages of Ladakh in northern India and the Karakoram of Pakistan, I left the mountain of Hugh's transparencies on the light table. It was one A.M., and I couldn't sleep. I lit up a kretek cigarette and climbed into a hammock strung by the guesthouse pool. The air was still and quite cool, the interstate nearly silent. This was my last night at Eric Hansen's house, where for the previous week I had sorted Hugh's slides. I inhaled the sweet clove smoke and listened to the gentle breeze in the avocado tree overhead. I sat there somewhere between reality and dream, between California poolside and Himalayan mountainside, and between present and past.

In the darkness I glanced at the open gate to my right and felt a presence. An unexpected and yet familiar guest. The long hours over the light table had lulled me into a trance not unlike that evoked by the shaman's drumbeat and incantations. I peered into the darkness. "Hugh?" I whispered.

Kevin Bubriski

102